WILDLIFE POACHING

WILDLIFE POACHING

LAURA OFFENHARTZ GREENE

A VENTURE BOOK

FRANKLIN WATTS
New York ■ Chicago ■ London ■ Toronto ■ Sydney

364.162
Gre

**THIS BOOK IS DEDICATED WITH LOVE TO
JESSICA RUTH GREENE, WHO AWAKENED MY
SOUL TO THE NATURAL WORLD.**

Photographs copyright ©: Photo Researchers, Inc.: pp. 13, 29 (both David Weintraub), 27 (National Archives), 33 (Will & Deni McIntyre), 41 (Stephan Krasemann), 51 top (Mitch Reardon) 99 (Okapia); UPI/Bettmann: p. 17; Visuals Unlimited: pp. 20 (John D. Cunningham), 65 (Leonard Lee Rue IV), 69 (W. A. Banaszewski), 89 (Bill Beatty); North Wind Picture Archives, Alfred, Me.: pp. 23, 95; Gamma-Liaison Inc.: pp. 37 (Francois Gilson), 54 (Wendy Stone), 62, 77 (both Wayne Miles), 115 (Stephen Ferry); Wide World Photos: pp. 45, 51 bottom, 86; Reuters/Bettmann: pp. 56, 59 bottom, 71, 104, 109; The Wildlife Collection/Martin Harvey: p. 59 top; U.S. Fish and Wildlife Service: p. 67; The Bettmann Archive: p. 73.

Library of Congress Cataloging-in-Publication Data

Greene, Laura.
Wildlife poaching / Laura Offenhartz Greene.
p. cm.—(A Venture book)
Includes bibliographical references and index.
ISBN 0-531-13007-X (lib. bdg.)
1. Poaching—Juvenile literature. [1. Poaching.] I. Title.
SK36.7.G74 1994
364.1'62—dc20 94-21035 CIP AC

Copyright © 1994 by Laura Offenhartz Greene
All rights reserved
Printed in the United States of America
6 5 4 3 2 1

ACKNOWLEDGMENTS

The author wishes to thank the following people and organizations for their time and generous help in the preparation of this book:

Ralph E. Christensen, director, Bureau of Law Enforcement, Division of Enforcement, State of Wisconsin, Department of Natural Resources, Madison, Wisconsin. Douglas D. Hoskins, Southeast District warden, law enforcement supervisor, State of Wisconsin Department of Natural Resources, Milwaukee, Wisconsin. National Parks and Conservation Association, Richard W. Risch, conservatory director, Milwaukee County Department of Parks, Recreation and Culture, Milwaukee, Wisconsin, Lucinda D. Schroeder, special agent, United States Department of the Interior, United States Fish and Wildlife Service, Division of Law Enforcement, Madison, Wisconsin. United States Fish and Wildlife Service, Madison, Wisconsin, for loan of numerous videotapes. Izzak Walton League. World Wildlife Fund.

And special thanks to two other people—my editor and friend, Henry Rasof, for his patience, encouragement, and help in making this manuscript better than it otherwise would have been; and my husband, Victor R. Greene, professor of history, University of Wisconsin at Milwaukee, for his assistance, wide-ranging knowledge, and love.

CONTENTS

CHAPTER **1**
POACHING: A BRIEF OVERVIEW
9

CHAPTER **2**
HISTORY AND LAWS
21

CHAPTER **3**
NORTH AMERICAN MAMMALS
31

CHAPTER **4**
MAMMALS OF AFRICA AND ASIA
48

CHAPTER **5**
BIRDS: DEAD OR ALIVE
63

CHAPTER **6**
SWIMMERS, SWARMERS, AND PLANTS
79

CHAPTER **7**
THE EFFECTS OF POACHING
92

CHAPTER **8**
CITIZENS AGAINST POACHING
102

CHAPTER **9**
PINCHERS AND POACHERS
113

SOURCE NOTES
125

FOR FURTHER READING
137

INDEX
139

CHAPTER

POACHING: A BRIEF OVERVIEW

In the days when the powerful and wealthy owned forests and everything in them, in a time when most people were poor and hungry, a man arose to fight for justice, freedom, and a fair distribution of natural resources. His name was Robin Hood. With the help of his Merrie Men, Robin Hood took game from Sherwood Forest, which belonged to the king of England, in order to feed the poor and bring about changes in the laws. The authorities called his acts poaching and declared Robin Hood an outlaw. Even though his motives were pure and his methods fair, in the eyes of the law, Robin Hood was a criminal. If caught, he would surely have been hanged. Robin Hood was one of England's beloved, legendary heroes and perhaps the world's most famous poacher.

Robin Hood's romantic exploits helped form people's attitudes toward poaching. Since the days of the renowned Merrie Men, the public sometimes tends to be sympathetic toward poachers who kill only for food or the protection of their livelihood. For example, in the winter of 1982, authorities looked the other way when poaching suddenly increased in Libby, Montana. Libby is a small town in the northwestern part of the state with a population of 3,500 and a timber-based economy. It was economically devastated when production of timber declined and the jobless rate reached 41 percent. Desiring to be self-sufficient, families began to live off the land. To survive, they hunted, fished, and grew their own vegetables. In a single month they poached forty moose from the surrounding woods. The previous monthly high had been eighteen. Although the poaching was illegal, there were no arrests.[1]

Poachers may be the economically deprived of any nation who seek to earn a meager living. In order to feed their families, unemployed Brazilians will poach and then sell endangered alligators, and African villagers will poach wild game for the same reason.[2]

When there is poverty and unemployment combined with ignorance of local laws and customs, poaching sometimes escalates. For example, in towns and cities across the United States poaching increased where recent Southeast Asian immigrants settled. It is common in some parts of the world, including Southeast Asia, for people to trap animals for meat. When Southeast Asian refugees emigrated to the United States in the 1970s and 1980s, they found it difficult to find work and viewed city parks as an ideal food source. This meant that in California, dinner for a newly arrived Laotian family often included squirrel, duck, stray dog, rat, or songbird.[3] In Utah, the meal for a poor Cambodian family was often porcupine, skunk, dove, woodpecker, robin, or baby bird, which had been obtained by poaching.[4]

While such poaching was illegal in both cases there were few arrests. In general, the game wardens believed that although these activities were unlawful, they were not grave crimes and these poachers did not constitute a major threat to the environment or the ecosystem. Instead of arresting the immigrants, government officials made an effort to educate them about American laws and customs. The authorities recognized that poverty had led the poachers to live off the land, just as Robin Hood had done in England, centuries before.

While some people may poach in order to eat, others poach in order to protect their income. For example, farmers and growers of livestock routinely kill wild animals to prevent them from ruining their cultivated land or attacking their domestic animals. In the United States ranchers shoot and poison wolves and birds, especially birds of prey, to prevent them from attacking their herds and eating their crops.

Today only a few poachers poach simply because they would go hungry otherwise—whether because they lacked food or the money to buy it. The majority poach because of greed. Most poachers regard the natural world as a source of personal profit. Their acts lead to the depletion of resources that belong to everyone.[5]

WHAT IS POACHING?

Poaching is the illegal act of killing, capturing, or removing mammals, birds, fish, reptiles, insects, or plants from their natural habitats. Governments have laws that put limits on the types and amounts of wildlife individuals may hunt. These laws determine the species that may be harvested, the number that may be taken, and the places where the hunts may occur. In addition there are laws that prohibit particular hunting methods. For instance, they prohibit the use of certain kinds of weapons or traps. Laws also protect many plants and other creatures (like butterflies) that we often may not think of as wildlife. Since most poaching includes animals, however, and vertebrates in particular, the term "poaching" is often used in this sense.

According to many people, most modern poachers are thieves who steal without regard to the pain and devastation they leave behind. It is common practice, for example, for many poachers to routinely use unethical methods to capture or kill their prey. These poachers may club animals to death or chase them from airplanes. They may take specific body parts, like bear gallbladders or paws, elephants' tusks, or rhinoceroses' horns, and leave the rest of the animal to rot. Duck poachers may scatter corn or other grain on the surface of a body of water in order to attract large numbers of birds for slaughter. Deer poachers may shine their car headlights or other lights at deer, then shoot them from moving vehicles. To many poachers, what matters most is the kill and the personal benefits they reap from it. Poachers give ethical hunters a bad reputation. While principled hunters engage in a fair chase and respect the law, the environment, and the wildlife, poachers do not.

WHO POACHES?

There is no such thing as a typical poacher. Poachers may be men or women; youngsters hunting with parents; or individuals alone or with groups, killing for "fun." Illegal hunters, fishers, bird and reptile catchers, and wildlife collectors come from all economic levels of society and are of many nationalities and professions. They may stalk their prey close to home or in foreign lands.

Poachers may be the ones who actually do the killing, the ones who arrange it (such as outfitters, hunting guides, and pilots) or among a variety of businesspeople who aid in the sale, transportation, or processing of wildlife or wildlife parts.

For example, outfitters arrange for the illegal hunts and help gunners get the supplies they require. Like guides or trackers, outfitters are businesspeople who may guarantee hunters a kill or even trophy-sized specimens. They often charge hunters thousands of dollars for the promise of a successful hunt. The only way to guarantee a kill is to engage in illegal hunting practices. Sometimes outfitters just buy dead animals from hunters and sell them to dealers who trade in animal parts. Some poachers play dual roles. Guides or trackers may also be outfitters or pilots. The pilot's job is to locate the particu-

Every year, game wardens confiscate thousands of illegal wildlife products.

lar animals that the hunters seek, then drive these animals to designated places for the kills. Pilots who do this are poachers just as the ones who pull the triggers are. Pilots not only drive animals but also help transport them. In Brazil, for example, a bush pilot can earn up to $1,500 a day flying alligator skins out of the country.[6]

Entrepreneurs cooperate with all of these people. It is they who arrange the transportation, smuggling, and sale of the wildlife. They work within the large, international network of illegal wildlife trafficking. This international network includes shopkeepers who knowingly sell poached animals and plants. The major difference between entrepreneurs and hunters in this network is that the former make more money.

WOODROW "TOMMY" BAGWELL

Poaching in Louisiana has been going on for generations. Woodrow "Tommy" Bagwell was a hard-core professional poacher from Morgan City, Louisiana. He saw no crime in poaching and felt no guilt when arrested for poaching. "I haven't done anything I'm really ashamed of," he said. "To me, if I steal from *someone* that's bad. But the good *Lord* put that game out there."[7]

Bagwell started poaching when he was fifteen years old, shooting rabbits and selling them for a dollar each. He never lacked for pocket money. In fact, he earned more money than his father, a laborer in a tool company, did. It was nothing for "Tommy" to kill a hundred rabbits in a night. He merely shone lights to freeze them, then blasted away.

In summers he and his friends poached as many as 2,000 pounds of catfish in a single night. They had no trouble catching these fish because they used a stunning device to shock them. Bagwell made it himself from an old crank-type telephone. The boys then sold the fish for thirty-five cents a pound—a bargain for the consumer and a bonanza for his friends and him.

It was deer hunting, however, that made Bagwell prosperous. By using a spotlight and a .22-caliber rifle he could effortlessly shoot the deer that gathered on high ground. One winter he killed 400 deer and sold them for thirty to seventy-five dollars each.

Bagwell never worried about game wardens, simply because he always had a boat that was faster than theirs and hunted in the bayou, a territory he knew like the back of his hand. However, the game wardens eventually caught up with and arrested him, not once but many times. Finally, as a repeat offender in fear of receiving longer jail sentences, he gave up poaching—or so he said.[8]

"CHARLEY PEACE" AND THE "RIVER RAT"

Charley Peace is quite a different sort of person. Some might call him a modern-day Robin Hood. He is an English gentleman whose dislike for the English aristocracy is so intense that he poaches only on the lands of earls. He is a cheerful rogue who enjoys poaching because it irritates landowners. His name, Charley Peace, is a pseudonym taken from a nineteenth-century cat burglar who never got caught.

Charley's methods are creative. For example, he uses wire snares and outfits his rifle with homemade silencers. He takes particular satisfaction in capturing pheasant, the pride of the earls' domains. He entices partridge with raisins threaded with horsehair. When the birds eat the raisin, the hairs get caught in their throats, leaving the birds flapping and therefore easily caught.

Charley's favorite weapon is a homemade hazelwood slingshot. He also uses homemade musket balls, and he frequently leaves one behind along with a dead bird as a sort of calling card to tease the earls' gamekeepers and let them know that Charley Peace was there. By selling poached game Charley can earn as much as $400 a week. In twenty-five years of poaching he has never been caught.[9]

On the other hand, some poachers are just small-time cheaters like the man who calls himself "the river rat." He has rotten, tobacco-stained teeth and lives in a shack on the banks of the Mississippi River. He, his wife, and his teenage son say they live on seventy-five dollars a month, the amount he earns by poaching game and selling it. His income stopped the moment he sold deer meat to two undercover federal wildlife agents. Despite the arrest, he didn't change his hunting habits.[10]

"BENNY" AND BILL

The poor poach for food and money, the rogues poach for fun, but the wealthy poach for sport and pride. One particular hunter comes from a well-to-do Louisiana family. He owns a successful towing company and rents 30,000 acres of land so that he, his friends, his family, and his business associates can go duck hunting on it. He hunts for sport, not money.

In December 1986 he was apprehended for poaching. It didn't matter that he was hunting on his own land. What mattered was that he shot fourteen ducks over the limit. When he was arrested he said, "I've always shot over the limit. . . . I've been taught since I was four years old to do it that way."[11] He expressed neither remorse nor anger.

A Texas banker longed for a pair of trophy-sized deer antlers but was unable to make the kill himself. Since he was a rather wealthy man, when given the opportunity, he bought the antlers of a white-tailed deer for $20,000. He then traveled to Mexico, shot a deer, and

This Michigan man has served time in jail for deer poaching, yet for him and many others, illegal hunting is the only way to provide enough food for their families.

had the purchased antlers mounted on the skull of the animal he shot. Next, he sent a phony story of his hunting prowess along with a picture of himself and the composite deer to *Outdoor Life,* which published the story.

Unfortunately for him, a Canadian law enforcement agent was reader of the magazine who read the article and saw the picture. He recognized the antlers, which were unusual because of their great size. They had been stolen from a Canadian taxidermy shop. The hunter was easily tracked down, convicted, and sentenced to five years' probation plus a $20,000 fine.[12] He, of course, is not a poacher, but his intense desire for a prizewinning rack is the kind of excessive passion that encourages poaching and helps to makes poaching profitable.

WHY PEOPLE POACH

The reasons for poaching are as diverse as the people who poach. Relatively few poachers engage in wildlife theft to avoid starvation. On the contrary, the justification for most poaching is far less innocent. A common motivation is the desire to win trophies or display animals' heads on walls. Some people poach in order to add rare butterflies or orchids to their private collections. Others poach for the recognition they receive when bragging to their peers about the number of birds or other animals they slew on a particular hunting trip. Still others engage in poaching simply because it is a part of their family's or community's tradition. The tradition may go back many generations, often a way of life handed down from parent to child. Finally, some people poach just for the "fun" of it.

There are those who poach because they believe they have a God-given right to take whatever the land has to offer. They believe strongly that no man-made law should infringe upon this right. They feel that whatever flies in the sky, swims in the waters, walks on the earth, or grows in the ground belongs to whoever can claim it.[13]

The main reason for poaching today, though, is money. Poaching has become a business and an international crime that is almost as profitable and well organized as the drug trade is. As in the drug trade, a hierarchy exists within this business. Those who receive the least amount of money have the most financial need. In this case it's the hunters. Each time the booty changes hands, its value increases. For example, a group of people in Africa with semiautomatic weapons, chain saws, and axes can lop off the horns of a rhinoceros and sell them for $1,000 a pair. This is big money for Africa's poor.[14] In Zimbabwe, "a poacher can make more money from a single rhino horn or a couple of elephant tusks than from a lifetime of farming."[15] However, by the time the horns and tusks reach their final destinations they can be worth $18,000 a pound, four times the price of gold. The demand for rhino horns for medicine or as status symbols is huge.[16]

A village family in Thailand can double its small annual income if one member nabs a bear and sells it. By the time the bear becomes the main course in a feast, albeit an illegal one, the dealer who arranged it has earned about $30,000. Each dinner guest may pay $500 to $600 a plate.[17]

WHAT IS POACHED?

Some people will poach any wildlife that has value, whether it lives above, below, within, or on the earth's surface. The more rare a species, the more expensive it becomes and the more earnestly it is sought, making it still more rare, more expensive, and more sought after.

The list of mammals that are illegally wild-caught and either traded live or as animal products is extensive. It includes such mammals as bears, cats, deer, elephants, fox, gibbons, monkeys, rhinoceroses, sheep, and wolves. The sought-after birds include birds of paradise, birds of prey (like falcons and owls), cockatoos, ducks, geese, parrots, and pheasant. Poachers also hunt reptiles such as alligators, crocodiles, iguanas, lizards, and snakes. Sea creatures like turtles and walrus also are commonly taken. In the plant kingdom the most com-

Many consumers who purchase wildlife products such as carved ivory or cheetah pelts may not realize that these items come from illegally poached animals.

monly poached species are the cactus, the orchid, and ginseng (an herb). Fish are not safe either, nor are insects (especially butterflies) or spiders.

Poachers work on every continent in the world and steal every form of wildlife. It makes no difference to them whether the quarry are in a national park, a protected game reserve, or on private property. It doesn't even matter to them how many of a particular species are left on this planet. What matters most to the poacher is "What's in it for me?"

CHAPTER

HISTORY AND LAWS

America has a hunting tradition that began in the days of the first settlers, when game was plentiful and the right to hunt was part of this nation's code of freedom. As the country became more populated, cities grew, daily life changed, and the wildlife population began to decline. In the eighteenth and nineteenth centuries, laws to protect animals were passed in order to preserve them for hunting, but even these laws were not enforced. Recognition of the need to protect wildlife for the sake of the earth's ecosystem was not widespread until the twentieth century. By then, not only had the number of species diminished, but the populations of existing species had declined as well.

HUNTING, PAST AND PRESENT

When the North American continent was settled by European colonists, most people fed their families from the land; hunting was an accepted part of life and there were few hunting laws. In the seventeenth century, settlers viewed animals as either food or "hellish fiends" to be destroyed. They found predators to be especially obnoxious.

By the eighteenth century, Americans were more enlightened. The general public no longer viewed animals as "spiritual threats." Although people still thought of animals that lived in the wild as "beasts," they generally were willing to accept the animal kingdom, provided it was "controlled." Killing predators at will was a way of controlling them.[1] For a long time there seemed to be no reason to limit hunting.

To most people living in the nineteenth century, wildlife still seemed plentiful, and as late as the Civil War many people still hunted for their food or their livelihood. Hunters routinely ignored the few hunting laws that existed. However, sometime during the century attitudes toward hunting and the environment began to change and hunting became a sport. At the same time, people began to see nature as a source of spiritual enrichment and knowledge.

As people moved into cities, they became more inclined to buy their meat rather than hunt for it. The farther away from the wilderness they lived, the more they valued the out-of-doors. They missed the open spaces, the clean air, the taste of wild meat, and the beauty of country landscapes. However, while many people became sensitive to nature's splendor and abundance, others began to abuse it.

More and more people began to enjoy wildlife in the city by means of fashion and cuisine. For example, women's hats increasingly were decorated with stuffed birds and feathers, and wild game became the preferred source of meat. In order to feed and dress the urban population, commercial hunting grew rapidly. Commercial, or market, hunting is the business of hunting wildlife for the purpose of selling food or ornaments to the nonhunting population.

In the nineteenth century, songbirds such as flickers, meadowlarks, bobolinks, passenger pigeons, and cedar waxwings were a regular part of the American diet. Robin soup was a gourmet's delight.[2] Even city people

During the nineteenth century, the abundant wildlife population provided Americans with ornamental feathers and exotic foods, and commercial hunting grew rapidly.

ate coot, quail, woodcock, twenty-six species of duck, bison, elk, caribou, muskrat, hare, and squirrel, to name only some species.[3] Holiday menus in fancy hotels included white-tailed-deer soup, broiled black bear, black-bear ragout, and antelope steak.[4] The result of the harvesting of these animals was a decline in game, but only the sport hunters noticed it. They became alarmed and were the first to worry about the seemingly indiscriminate killing for fun, food, or fashion. For the most part, this hunting was perfectly legal, and therefore not poaching.

Sport hunters thought that animals were worth saving at a time when most Americans either didn't care or thought of animals as dispensable.[5] In fact, it was mainly the sport hunters who initiated the conservation movement. They organized, lobbied for change, and worked toward the establishment of national parks. They considered the preserves and national parks to be the only way of protecting the wilderness from market hunters, loggers, and sawmill operators.[6] They wanted to save the wildlife for sport hunting. In 1872 Congress established Yellowstone National Park as the first of its kind and set limits on market hunting. However, Yellowstone continued to be a bonanza for market hunters until 1886 when federal agents went into the park to enforce the laws and prevent poaching.[7]

The most prominent sportspeople in the conservation movement were George Bird Grinnel, hunter, fisherman, editor of *Forest and Stream,* and founder of the Audubon Society; and Theodore Roosevelt, the enthusiastic big-game hunter who was also the twenty-sixth president of the United States. They were charter members of the Boone and Crockett Club, a hunting club established in 1887 and dedicated, at least in the first few decades of its existence, to the preservation of wildlife. Club members lobbied for strict penalties against poachers, established a sportsman's code, and worked hard to educate hunters to use, not abuse, the nation's natural resources. The code emphasized the "fair chase" and prohibited practices such as shooting animals at night or those that were immobilized in snow or were swimming.[8] In the eighteenth, nineteenth, and early twentieth centuries the few laws that were passed were either not enforced or simply ignored.

TO WHOM DO THE LAND AND ITS WILDLIFE BELONG?

Between 1901 and 1909, during the presidency of Theodore Roosevelt, Congress declared that 125 million acres of land would be designated national forests and parks. One problem resulting from this was that much of this land already belonged to private individuals. The government did not offer the owners fair compensation in return, but simply appropriated the land. The problem continues to the present day. Many of the original owners or their heirs continue to claim ownership. They believe it was wrong for the government to take it and wrong for the government to prohibit hunting—especially *their* hunting—on land they regard as their own.

The Buckfield family of Graham County, North Carolina, for example, insist that they own 5,555 acres of Great Smoky Mountains National Park. The Buckfields say the government stole their land when it created the park. Family members expect to continue hunting at will, even though they are frequently fined for poaching.[9]

Attitudes toward hunting have changed a great deal since the days when most people lived off the land. The problem of who owns the land and the wildlife on it, and in what manner the wildlife may be taken, is a complex one. Conservationists and proponents of animal rights say future generations of humans own the wetlands, the parks, the forests, and all the wildlife within them. They argue that humanity must protect the planet's natural resources for we are all bound into an interdependent system. Many of these people would prohibit hunting entirely if they could. They stigmatize hunting as a bloodthirsty activity, unworthy of humanity, and see hunters as the enemy.

Ethical hunters resent the accusations. They protest

that the land and all that's on it belong to those who choose to use it. In fact, they declare that hunting fees and taxes on guns and ammunition support the parks and wildlife recreation areas and make them available for public use.

MAJOR LEGISLATION

Early in President Theodore Roosevelt's term of office and with his encouragement, Congress passed the Lacey Act of 1900. It was the first significant legislation to protect wildlife in the United States. Even today the Lacey Act, with its many amendments, continues to impose penalties for the "wanton destruction" of animals and to prohibit interstate shipment of wildlife and wildlife products taken in violation of the law. The act began by forbidding market hunting—the business of killing wildlife for profit—and the interstate shipment of wildlife and wildlife products taken in violation of state laws. The act was then expanded to make it a federal crime to import species that had been taken, transported, or sold in violation of foreign laws as well. Today the Lacey Act forbids even the *possession* of illegal species.

The second crucial piece of legislation came in 1917 with the passage of the Migratory Birds Treaty between the United States and Canada. The treaty outlaws the spring hunting of migratory birds, imposes bag limits on designated species, and prohibits hunters from indiscriminately destroying nests and eggs, practices commonly engaged in for generations. As part of the requirements of the treaty, the signatory governments drew up a list of birds that could not be sold or traded internationally.

The treaty has been amended numerous times over the past seventy-five years in a continuing effort to protect threatened (at risk of becoming endangered) and endangered (at risk of becoming extinct) migratory birds.

During the administration of President Theodore Roosevelt, significant legislation protecting wildlife in the United States was passed for the first time.

Periodically the treaty is revised so that as migratory bird populations dwindle or become restored, the number of species on the protected list increases or decreases.

In conjunction with this treaty the United States passed additional legislation known as the Federal Migratory Birds Act. This law distinguishes game birds, which hunters may shoot, from nongame birds, which they may not shoot. Many nations have similar laws.

The next significant piece of legislation was the Endangered Species Act, first passed in 1966 and, like the other protective legislation, amended several times. The Endangered Species Act prohibits most people from importing and exporting species listed as endangered or threatened. On a limited basis and under certain specified conditions, people may still import threatened species. Scientists and zoo managers, for example, have special importing privileges. The U.S. Fish and Wildlife Service revises the list of endangered and threatened species regularly by conducting its own research and reviewing petitions from interested groups and foreign countries.

In 1972 Congress passed the Marine Mammal Protection Act, which prohibits the importation of such marine mammals as whales, narwhals, walruses, polar bears, sea lions, and sea otters, as well as their parts and products.

One of the most important agreements affecting international trade in wildlife is the Convention on International Trade in Endangered Species (CITES), a comprehensive treaty first signed in 1975 by 109 nations, including the United States. In subsequent years the number of signers and protected species has grown. CITES regulates and in some cases prohibits people from importing and exporting certain wildlife species. Repre-

Legislation such as the Endangered Species Act in 1966 and the Convention on International Trade in Endangered Species in 1975 prohibits the import or export of these wildlife products, which are destined for sale as "hunting trophies."

sentatives of the signatory nations meet every two years and decide upon the list of animals and plants whose trade they want to regulate or ban. Unfortunately, the signatory nations do not always enforce these regulations.

The most recent piece of animal protection legislation in the United States is the Wild Bird Conservation Act of 1992, which provides varying levels of protection for different classes of birds. Congress imposed an immediate ban on the importation of wild bird species thought to be most imperiled. In 1993 the ban was extended to birds that CITES lists as threatened.

Hunters, nonhunters, and legislators are likely to disagree over which species hunters may stalk and how many of a particular species it is appropriate to kill at one time. They probably will also disagree over the suitable times and places that hunting may occur. In the end, the law will determine the rules, and those who break the law are poachers and are subject to prosecution.

CHAPTER

NORTH AMERICAN MAMMALS

Among the most beautiful and sought after of nature's creatures are big-game mammals. In North America, big-game mammals such as deer, elks, moose, and bears have aesthetic, scientific, ecologic, and economic value. They are sought after by various groups of people, including nature lovers, hunters, scientists, and poachers.

Why are these animals poached and who poaches them? They are poached for food, for sport, for "thrills," for money, and for trophies. The most serious kind of poaching is done by market hunters who engage in large-scale killing for resale and profit. Although market hunting has been illegal in the United States since 1900, today it is a thriving industry.[1] Bears are the most sought-after big-game mammals, but elks, walrus, sheep, antelope, and deer also are targets of such hunters.

BEARS

Bears, powerful animals high up in the food chain, were at one time fairly widely distributed and had few rivals for food and territory. Encroached upon by humans, their numbers and territories have dwindled significantly in the United States and abroad. According to Bill Cook, an agent with the National Park Service, poachers consider the bear "a marketable commodity and they broker its parts to the highest bidder...."[2] The scarcity of bears combined with the fact that certain of their parts are very valuable, has led to intense poaching of these animals. The financial rewards are great, and the risk of getting caught is minimal.

For something to be valuable, it must be in demand, it must be extremely desirable, and it must be in short supply. This combination creates a tremendous incentive for people to obtain the item at almost any price. Bears constitute such a commodity.

One of the biggest markets for bears and bear products is Asia, where in countries like China, North Korea, and South Korea bears' gallbladders and galls are believed to be good for the human body. Depending upon the size, sex, and season, a bear's gallbladder can weigh between 1 and 35 grams and contain between 1 teaspoonful and 1 quart of liquid gall, or bile. Since Asian bears are on the brink of extinction, individuals in search of bears' gall and other bear products have turned to black bears in the United States for their supply.

Bears' gall is said to cure blood poisoning, backaches, and eye problems. Some claim it will cure indigestion, fever, hemorrhoids, and heart disease.[3] Bears' gall is sometimes used to increase stamina, stimulate sex drive, and improve overall health. Many people take daily doses of it the way Americans take multiple vitamins.[4] Although belief in the curative power of bear gall dates back about 4,500 years,[5] there is no scientific evidence that the gallbladder or gall has any of these effects.

Bears' gall is also marketed to non-Asians. A reporter visiting a major hotel in Tianjin, China, saw a row of boxes containing red capsules. Above the boxes was a handwritten sign in English: "Bear's Gall Pills good for relieving internal heat, pains and nebular. It can be used for treatment of swelling and pain in the eyes, photophobia and . . . tears caused by excessive internal heat."[6]

Although many Asians find medicinal or aphrodisiacal value in wildlife products, the positive effects of bears' gall or rhinos' horns have never been proved. Pictured here, among other ingredients, are a deer's skull (center), bears' gall (top), and freshwater pearls (lower right).

How valuable is a bear's gallbladder or its gall? One bear's gallbladder that is intact can sell for as much as $5,000 in China, Japan, or Korea.[7] Sometimes bears' gallbladders are literally worth more than their weight in gold![8] As with street drugs, such as heroin, the cost can vary markedly. As of September 1993 it was $360 per ounce. In Japan they have sold for more than $1,800 an ounce.[9] According to a 1991 report in *National Geographic,* a businessperson in South Korea made the front page of the *Korean Herald* for importing thirty-five frozen black bears and selling their gallbladders for $18,300 each.[10] Gall can sell for as much as seventy dollars for 1 teaspoonful.[11]

In 1989, agents in Massachusetts, Connecticut, New York, and Florida tracked the slaughter of 400 bears in transactions worth $50,000.[12] In 1990 Arizona agents confiscated 200,000 bears' gall pills. They were laced with fillers just as cocaine and heroin are laced by dealers. The market value of these pills was $26,000.[13]

Other parts of the bear—including the meat, claws, blood, hides, and teeth—are also much sought after. Bears' meat is either a delicacy or a staple, depending on the consumer. The meat is a favored dish not only in Asia but also in America.[14] For some, bears' liver is a special treat. Bear-paw soup is said to impart strength and fertility.[15] A single serving of bear paw soup has sold for as much as $100 in South Korea and $800 in Japan.[16] Bears' blood can be drunk as a beverage.[17] Consumers around the world buy bears' hides for rugs and wear their teeth and claws as jewelry.[18]

Bears—especially grizzlies, which are much larger and more fearsome than black bears—are also sought, both legally and illegally, for trophies by wealthy sport hunters and other individuals. Although they seek no material profit for their specimens, their quests for trophies are certainly based on greed of a different sort. Those who help them legally or illegally to obtain grizzly bears may earn thousands of dollars.[19] Even if the buyers do not do the actual poaching, they are accessories to the acts and as guilty as the hunters who do the killing and trafficking.

Bears' gall has become so valuable, and bears so

hard to get, that substitutions for bears' gallbladders and gall (for example, pigs' gallbladders and gall) have flooded the market. To demonstrate the authenticity of the bears' gallbladders that they sell, some dealers prepare the bears under the customer's watchful eye, and deliver the gallbladder in person. They kill the bears by dropping them into a tub of hot water, slice open their bodies, remove their gallbladders, and hand them over to the buyers. The combination of rich people who want fresh bears' gall or gallbladders, and the availability of substitutions, has helped make the real thing even more desirable and expensive.

Bear poaching became a recognized problem in 1981, when California Fish and Wild Life agents broke up a black bear poaching ring and recovered 187 bear paws and gallbladders destined for sale in Hong Kong and China.[20] Since that time, federal agents have documented the growing problem. For example, a three-year undercover operation ended in 1988, when law enforcement officials arrested forty-three people in Knoxville, Tennessee, for selling 266 gallbladders, 85 claws, 77 feet, 4 heads, 9 hides and 1 live bear to federal agents posing as merchants.[21]

It is not hard for bear hunters to be considered bear poachers in the United States. Although a number of states allow bear hunting, often it is by special permit because of the small number of bears left in the wild. In addition, legal hunters may be prohibited from selling any parts of the bear. These laws vary from state to state. In Montana, for example, it is legal to hunt bears during a limited season, but illegal to sell their gallbladders. On the other hand, in California, Oregon, and Washington, it is illegal to sell *any* bear parts.

Craig Boheler, a Wyoming hunter, finds such laws hypocritical. "If there's anyone who's against poaching, I am," he said, "but as long as it's legally harvested, I just can't see leaving a couple hundred dollars to rot in the forest."[22] Would allowing *legal* bear hunters to sell bears' gall, claws, skins, or meat increase the supply enough to lower the demand, in turn lowering the price that illegal bear products command on the market and reduce the incentive to poach? This question perhaps needs to be investigated as part of a solution to the problem.

Poachers use various methods, new and old, to track and kill bears. Ricken M. Brame, director of the North Carolina Wildlife Federation, reported how poachers tracked a pregnant bear through a radio transmitter planted on her by researchers. "She had no chance. She was denning—woozy as if she was under anesthesia. . . . It was like shooting a baby in a crib."[23] Other poachers train dogs to kill bears. They would do this by chaining a live bear to a tree and then encouraging their dogs to attack and kill the animal.[24]

Once the dogs are properly trained, the poachers fit them out with radio collars and set them loose to track and kill bears. The dogs will either tree the bears or attack them while they are sleeping in their winter dens. The poachers then locate the dogs by means of the radio signal, take the bears' gallbladders, and then leave the rest of the bear behind.[25] Trophy hunters may hire outfitters, guides, or pilots to locate a bear and then chase it by airplane to where the hunter stands ready for the kill.[26]

"Bear hunters are tough people," says Warden Roger D. Gibby, a North Carolina game warden. "These people are slobs, they are not real hunters," says Colonel Gerald Simmons, chief of law enforcement for the Virginia Commission of Game and Inland Fisheries.[27] Even cubs are killed for their parts.[28] Game wardens in Washington State have found bears stuffed in dumpsters, their paws and gallbladders gone.[29]

No one knows how many bears are left in the United States. The U.S. Fish and Wildlife Services have determined that in many areas bears are threatened with ex-

Many poachers chain bears to trees and encourage their dogs to attack them. The bears are then decapitated and stripped of their pelts and gallbladders. This practice is common in both Europe and North America.

tinction. Although bears can live as long as twenty years, the life spans of those in the southern Appalachian Mountains are on average only six years. In Katmai National Park in Alaska (a four-million-acre preserve that has become one of the most popular bear-hunting areas in the state), bears have visibly decreased in size over the past decade. All the large ones have been killed.[30]

In 1989, the National Audubon Society estimated that only 400 to 600 bears remained in Great Smoky Mountains National Park, a park in which some remote campsites have bear-proof compounds. Some experts have estimated that only 500 bears remain in Florida. Alarmed at the figure, a Florida congressional delegation asked the U.S. Fish and Wildlife Services to protect the bears and prohibit hunting. Yet hunting continues. As few as 5,000 bears remain in Colorado.[31] Ray Bane, Katmai National Park superintendent, said, "Those bears out there are not being hunted . . . they're essentially being butchered."[32]

In response to the demand for bears' gall and gallbladders, efforts are being made to produce bears' gall synthetically. In addition, bears are now being raised on game farms. In North Korea, South Korea, and China plastic hoses are surgically implanted into living bears and their bile is collected in small plastic bags, assuring a renewable stock of this valuable product. This method makes killing the bears unnecessary. Instead, the animals are kept in small cages. Unfortunately, many of these bears have been poached from the United States.

Some people have suggested that if such game farms could be made self-sustaining, and if they could produce enough bears' gall for the market, perhaps the need for poached bears would decline significantly. However, lower prices might lead to increased demand for bears' gall and gallbladders, jacking up the prices and contributing to a vicious cycle whose end result might spell even greater disaster for the bear population.

ELK

Elk are another legally hunted North American mammal. They are related to the deer and are native to both Europe and the United States. At one time elk could be found over most of the United States and southern Canada. Hunting and the loss of feeding areas have reduced their population so that most of the remaining elks now live in the Rocky Mountain chain with a large herd in Yellowstone National Park.

Elks are shy animals that live in herds, each composed of a single male and several females. A full-grown bull (male) elk stands about 5 feet (1.5 m) high at the shoulder, and its rounded antlers may have twelve or more points and a spread of about 5 feet (1.5 m) at its widest part. Since there are fewer elks than there are deer, there is an incentive for sport hunters to try to bag them. Sport hunters seek elks for their heads or racks of antlers, which they hang on the walls of their homes. Trophy-sized racks and heads increase in value over time, as antiques do.[33] Some are worth thousands of dollars.

As with bears, however, the biggest threat to elks comes not from ordinary sport hunters but from poachers. And elks, like bears, are sought for their medicinal and trophy value. Elk poachers hunt and kill as many elks as they can find and sell the antlers either to hunters who claim them as their own or to traders who sell them, often to citizens of some Asian countries, to use as an aphrodisiac or medicines to ward off flu and colds.[34]

When elk antlers are in the velvet stage (covered with soft, hairy skin and filled with blood, which nourishes them and protects them as they grow) they are worth as much as $140 a pound. People who use elk antler as an aphrodisiac or medicine may consume the blood squeezed from the horns, or ingest powdered horn, or thinly sliced horn.

The powder or slices are sometimes boiled with herbs such as ginseng, an important herb in Asian medicine.[35] As with bears' gall and gallbladders, there is no scientific evidence that elks' horns have aphrodisiacal or medicinal properties. There is no scientific evidence, in fact, that *any* substance is an aphrodisiac.

The methods used to take elk's antlers are as gruesome as those used to take bears' gallbladders. Poachers often kill the elk, sever their heads with chain saws, carry the antlers away, and leave the rest of their carcasses to rot.[36]

Live elk sell for $16,000 a head. Since elk produce new antlers each year, some people have begun farming elk. Owners of elk farms simply cut off the antlers whenever they choose to and sell them. Sometimes the size of a farm herd is increased through poaching additional elks from the wilderness. Although raising elks on farms is legal, many people believe that this will just encourage poaching.[37]

Antlers shed naturally in places like Rocky Mountain National Park in Colorado or the National Elk Preserve near Yellowstone National Park in Montana, where many elks live, may not be gathered but must remain where they fall as part of the natural ecosystem. Yet poachers prefer to poach antlers from national parks and forests because the forage there has no chemicals.[38]

WALRUS

Walrus are large sea mammals. For centuries Eskimos have hunted them for food, hides, tusks, and blubber. Walrus resemble seals except they have canine teeth, or tusks, which seals do not. The tusks project downward from their upper jaws and in a full-grown walrus of either sex the tusks may be as long as 30 inches (76 cm). Walrus use these tusks to dig food from the ocean floor. They live in small herds near the North Pole, and although

Many walrus are slaughtered for their tusks, which are an excellent source for ivory.

they frequent coastal islands and shores, for the most part they dwell on drifting pack ice. Unless attacked, walrus tend to be docile animals.

When the international community banned the sale of ivory in order to save the elephant from extinction, hunters turned to the walrus as the next-best ivory source. The kill got so large that walrus are now a protected species. Only Native Americans—Eskimos, in particular—are permitted to hunt or sell them. The government granted this permission in 1972 to help preserve the Eskimo culture. The law states that Eskimos are allowed to kill as many walrus as they need, provided they do so in a nonwasteful manner; in other words, they are supposed to use all parts of these animals.

However, since 1972 times have changed for the Eskimos. For one thing, they do not require walrus for meat and clothing as much as they once did. Therefore, most Eskimos walrus hunters kill for ivory; the meat and other body parts are of secondary value. In Anchorage, Alaska, for example, raw ivory changes hands in much the same way as currency does. People use it to buy gas, groceries, drugs, and liquor.[39]

Although most Eskimos follow the spirit of the law, some do not and so would seem to be poaching. New methods of killing walrus also suggest poaching rather than nonwasteful hunting. Although Eskimos still use their traditional skin boats for hunting, they are unlikely to use traditional handmade harpoons. Instead, some now use automatic weapons. And instead of going after one or a few walrus at a time, with automatic weapons they can attack an entire herd, with ivory the main motive for such killing.

Like poachers of bears and elk, walrus poachers—Eskimos and non-Eskimos alike—often chop off the animals' heads for the tusks and dump the headless bodies into the sea. Sometimes poachers shoot so many of these sea mammals that the animals sink into the sea before their heads can be retrieved. In the spring, the dead walrus both with and without heads wash up onto shore.[40] When hunters are able to, they also will lop off the walrus's penis. The carved and polished penis bones, called *oozíks* by the Eskimos, are used as conversation pieces by peoples of many nationalities.[41]

Most walrus poachers are said to be primarily from the northern Alaskan towns of Nome, Gambell, and Savoonga along the Bering Sea and Wales on the Chukchi Sea. There they hunt walrus "almost solely for their tusks."[42] They sell the ivory in exchange for cocaine or marijuana.[43] The ivory winds up in international markets as status symbols such as carved objects of art and jewelry. The demand for ivory has increased so much that biologists warn that the number of animals killed each year is two or three times the rate at which they can reproduce.[44]

Of course, not all Eskimo walrus hunters are poachers, nor are all walrus poachers Eskimos. Most Eskimos cooperate with the United States Fish and Wildlife Services and are eager to end the slaughter.

BIGHORN SHEEP

Bighorn sheep live in mountain regions where the steep terrain makes it difficult for people to go. These surefooted animals can race up and down slopes that are hundreds of feet high. Even the young ones can jump from rock to rock with the grace of a gymnast. Since bighorn sheep are so difficult to reach, it is an enormous challenge for game hunters to bag even one. Wild sheep are not valued for their wool, are not claimed to have medicinal value, and are not particularly tasty to humans. However, they do have curved horns that can measure up to 4 feet (1.2 m) long with a spread of about 2 feet (0.6 m). These horns are what hunters seek.

The main motive for killing wild sheep is to possess their horns, which can win hunting trophies. These trophies are so important to some hunters that they frequently use illegal methods, such as shooting at the sheep from helicopters.[45] When a hunter kills what is called "a complete set," that is, a Dall, a Rocky Mountain bighorn, a desert bighorn, and a Stone sheep, he or she may earn a trophy. Collecting hunting trophies is like collecting art. As the years pass and the animals become more rare, the trophies increase in value.[46] A complete set of heads brings a black-market price of about

$50,000. The larger the heads, the more they are worth.[47]

As so few Dall sheep remain, legal hunting of them is extremely limited. The government auctions the permits to hunt them. In 1987 one permit went for $91,000,[48] but by 1991 a hunter willingly paid $100,000 for a permit.[49]

DEER

About sixty species of deer exist throughout the world. White-tailed deer (also called Virginia deer) are the most common big-game animal in North America. They are so plentiful in many areas of the country that hunting them is commonplace and licenses to do so are easy to obtain. According to some estimates, legal hunters kill about three million deer annually.[50]

Nevertheless poaching is a persistent problem, especially since most states limit the number of deer that can be taken in a season. Even some hunters who oppose poaching bears, walrus, and elk see little wrong with deer poaching. Since deer are not in danger of extinction, at least nationwide, they see no problem in killing more than the legal limit. They sometimes argue that if hunters didn't hunt the deer, these animals would die of starvation. Hunting, they say, is the kind thing to do and is necessary to control overpopulation. Environmentalists, conservationists, and animal-rights groups, however, reply that even though we have killed most of the predators, nature can still control the deer population if we stop meddling. Natural factors such as extreme weather and availability of food can bring balance to the population. The natural birth rate slows in times of stress.

Many hunters break deer hunting laws. Some are market hunters who poach to make money. They sell the meat to restaurants, private clubs, or even low-income

Although it is lawful to hunt deer, many poachers kill over the legal limit and sell the meat to restaurants and dinner clubs. Here, poachers have taken the carcasses and left the heads behind.

families as an inexpensive source of food.[51] Others kill simply because they like to bag deer. "It's fun," said one poacher.[52] In Salt Lake City, Utah, for example, officials caught poachers killing deer that gathered at feeding stations established by donations collected to feed these animals during a harsh winter. The animals were shot "for the thrill."[53]

Other poachers kill for trophies. In Santa Clara, New York, the desire for a trophy motivated a hunter to kill a white-tailed deer on a private estate in the Adirondack Mountains. The deer's antlers were huge. They weighed 219 pounds (99 kg) and would have been a prize kill if the authorities had not charged him with trespassing and confiscated the antlers.[54]

Wherever there are deer, there is deer poaching. Some hunters continue to take what they please. A few hunters feel it is their right to do so. The legal limit on the number of deer that may be shot varies considerably from state to state and season to season. Each year the people who manage the nation's natural resources determine these limits. They base their decisions on the size and health of the deer population. For example, in some years in one state a hunter may legally kill only one deer with a bow and arrow and one deer with firearms, but in another state a hunter might be allowed to kill more. Sometimes hunters may purchase special permits to bag extra deer. The bag limit may go as high as twelve or more. Hunters, however, do not always obey the limits. According to one report a single deer poacher might take as many as 100 deer illegally in a season.[55] In Southington, Connecticut, state environmental officers raided a slaughterhouse and found twenty poached deer carcasses in the walk-in freezer. Authorities estimated that that many were poached each week.[56]

Poaching methods are well documented. Many poachers shoot from moving vehicles on back roads during illegal deer chases. Some hunters, out for a thrill, think nothing of shooting out of the window of their automobile. Normally, hunting is illegal at night, but that is when much poaching is done. Poachers may shine bright lights, which freeze the deer in their tracks, making them easy targets. This practice is so common that it has many names, depending on where it is done. *Spotlighting, firehunting, jacklighting,* and *jacking deer* are a few such names.

Some poachers use infrared lights to hunt deer at night, while others use nightscopes to improve their accuracy. Some even monitor radio frequencies used by biologists, employees of conservation organizations, and law enforcement agencies to help them locate deer or avoid detection.

All in all, poaching of big-game mammals, whether for financial reward, for "sport" and trophies, for food, for thrills, or for some other reason, is a serious problem in the United States. In some locales, where once-abundant deer populations have been decimated, law enforcement officials compare the effects of poaching to those of a wildlife epidemic.

CHAPTER

MAMMALS OF AFRICA AND ASIA

In Africa and Asia the black market in animals and animal products is a thriving industry. Most of the illegal wildlife shipments go through the ports of Hong Kong and Thailand to destinations all over the world, including the United States. The impact of wildlife poaching has been devastating to many mammal species. If the population density of an animal species isn't high enough, the males and females have a hard time finding each other in order to mate. In addition, with fewer animals available, there is a smaller gene pool, which tends to produce a weaker species. Animals like the elephant, black rhinoceros, tiger, chimpanzee, and gibbon are in danger of extinction. However, as long as prices are high, people will poach, continuing to remove animals—dead or alive—from their native habitats.

AFRICAN ELEPHANTS

Millions of elephants once roamed the vast areas of Asia, Africa, and India. At one time 350 different species may have existed. Today most of the world's remaining elephants are in Africa, concentrated in wildlife sanctuaries, where hunting is forbidden. However, the killing continues. In the 1980s there were 1.3 million elephants in Africa. Today there are fewer than 625,000.[1]

An alarming drop in the elephant population took place in the 1960s and 1970s. There were many reasons for the decline. Drought and habitat reduction caused some of the population to diminish, as did hunting by sport hunters and by poor people (who killed for food). Another cause was the illegal shooting of elephants by farmers and property owners because these animals were a nuisance in their fields and villages. Most of the killing, however, was done by poachers for ivory, the material of elephant tusks.

In the 1970s the wars in Uganda, Angola, Namibia, and Mozambique made Africans living in these countries desperate for money.[2] The temptation to kill elephants for their ivory tusks was strong. These mammals were an easy target, and poachers could sell the ivory for a great deal of money. In the early 1970s a good pair of tusks sold for several thousand dollars.[3] As elephants became more difficult to find, the price of ivory rose and the killing increased. By the end of the decade, a single tusk weighing between 90 and 130 pounds (40 and 59 kg) sold for $82 a pound.[4]

By far the largest single group of poachers were Idi Amin's Ugandan army. Idi Amin, the military dictator of Uganda between 1972 and 1979, encouraged the killing. Not only did the ivory bring money, but the activity amused his men. During those years his soldiers killed an estimated 9,000 elephants in Kabalega National Park alone.[5]

Zoologists and conservationists had been worried about the demise of elephants for some time, but nothing was done until after the collapse of the Amin government. In 1980 Iain Douglas-Hamilton, a Scottish zoologist and a well-known elephant expert, brought the seriousness of the problem to light. Douglas-Hamilton obtained financial assistance from the World Wildlife Fund and the new Ugandan government in order to take an aerial census of the Ugandan elephant population. The census confirmed what he already suspected: elephants were in danger of extinction. He found that while in 1972 15,000 elephants were in Kabalega National Park, by 1980 only 850 remained. He warned the public that if the trend continued, elephants would soon disappear from the earth.[6] Although the problem received publicity, little was done.

Despite the warning that elephants were in danger of extinction, poachers continued to kill them. In fact, the killing increased after Idi Amin's overthrow. As his soldiers retreated to Sudan and Zaire, they killed more elephants. A 1982 *Washington Post* article reported that ivory poaching cost the lives of 50,000 to 150,000 elephants a year, and the number continued to climb.[7] In the eight years between 1979 and 1987 poachers slaughtered 400,000 more elephants and in the process obtained 3,900 tons of ivory.[8]

Through the years newspaper articles sporadically reported this news. For example, a 1982 article in the *Christian Science Monitor* warned that the Namibian elephant was near extinction. Only 84 remained alive in 1982. Experts feared the worst. The Namibian elephant is unique. It has bigger, tougher feet than other elephants, enabling it to walk on both sand and rocks.[9]

Despite the publicity, poaching continued. Some of the poachers were based in Mozambique. They regularly crossed their northeast border into South Africa. In a period of eighteen months, which ended in December 1982, poachers got tusks worth $500,000 from South Africa's Kruger National Park, one of the world's largest wildlife sanctuaries. Poachers targeted bulls for their ivory but indiscriminately killed cows and calves as well.[10]

In the 1970s and 1980s the international demand for ivory was enormous. People were willing to pay large sums of money for ivory bracelets, necklaces, chess pieces, figurines, hair combs, shoehorns, daggers, billiard balls, piano keys, ice buckets, and buttons.[11] Few

(Left): Every year, poachers murder thousands of African elephants for their ivory tusks and leave their carcasses for the vultures. *(Below):* Namibian officials stand over the largest recorded ivory haul, which was intercepted as poachers tried to smuggle it out of the country.

buyers thought about where the ivory came from or how it was obtained. Consumers didn't seem to connect the products they bought with what was happening to the great beast from which they came, and sellers didn't care.

The situation, however, was not entirely hopeless. From time to time someone cared enough to take action. For example, in March 1985, a villager from Nairobi, the capital of Kenya, informed authorities where they could find 924 tusks. He had discovered that poachers had stashed them in the Bothei forest near Nairobi. They had a market value of $300,000.[12]

Rampant elephant poaching continued for years. The problem extended throughout Africa, and its governments could do little to solve it. As the elephant population dwindled, the price of their tusks rose. It therefore became more and more profitable to kill elephants. African citizens needed the cash.

Another reason for the governments' lack of success in solving the problem was that while poachers were armed with automatic rifles, the rangers were poorly equipped. The few weapons supplied to the rangers frequently misfired, and their vehicles often failed to start. Still another reason was that the rangers were poorly paid and therefore easily bribed. Corruption among African park authorities was rampant.[13] By 1988, poachers were traveling in gangs as large as fifty and ambushing government patrols. They even assaulted tourists.[14] Newspapers reported the growing number of incidents far and wide.

In 1988, in Kenya, Richard Leakey, the world-famous paleontologist, who at the time was head of Kenya's wildlife department and chairman of the East African Wildlife Society, a private organization working to preserve African wildlife, called elephant poaching a "growing national crisis—economic sabotage with far reaching and lasting effect on the stability and success of this country."[15] Leakey was worried not only about elephants but also about tourism and the effect that the loss of Kenya's wild animals would have on visitors.

Leakey warned Daniel Moi, president of Kenya, in 1988 that the nation was losing 150 elephants a week to poachers, with the result that the nation's elephant population had declined 85 percent in fifteen years.[16] President Moi trusted Leakey and decided that drastic measures had to be taken at once. He issued an order that poachers were to be shot on sight, and he dismissed many government officials in an effort to put an end to corruption. Despite his actions, however, the poaching continued. Poachers were willing to risk their lives for the potential financial reward. Even sport hunters, thrilled by the added risk, continued to poach elephants. Soon after Moi's announcement, newspapers reported that nine Arab sheiks, with the help of Kenyan government officials, had illegally killed 200 wild animals on a single hunting trip.[17]

President Moi and Leakey were desperate. The extinction of the elephants in Kenya seemed frighteningly imminent. In order to call attention to the problem, in July 1989 Leakey and President Moi set fire to 12 tons of confiscated ivory. The ivory was worth $3 million, money that the Kenyan government badly needed. It was a dramatic effort to show the world that the slaughter had to stop. It was also a plea for help.[18]

The conflagration had the desired effect. In October 1989, 103 nations, signers of the Convention on International Trade in Endangered Species (CITES), agreed to ban trade in ivory. By that time, however, Kenya, Sudan, and Tanzania had lost 80 percent of their herds; Somalia and Uganda, 90 percent; and the nations of central Africa, 33 percent.[19] The ban agreement was a start, but it was not enough.

Japan, by far the largest buyer of ivory, and Hong Kong, one of the centers of the ivory trade, would not go

World-famous paleontologist Dr. Richard Leakey played a crucial role in publicizing the plight of Kenya's elephant population. In 1989, he and Kenya's president, Daniel Moi, had 12 tons of ivory incinerated to show that the slaughter had to stop.

along with the ban, although both countries promised to limit their ivory imports. Japan based its refusal on its desire to help the nations in southern Africa: an international ban on the sale of ivory would be a disservice to these nations that managed elephant herds as crops and harvested elephant tusks to benefit their economies.[20] All in all, sixty nations refused to sign the agreement, among them South Korea, Taiwan, and many African countries that resented the interference by whites in their internal affairs.[21] African countries like Somalia and Burundi signed the CITES agreement but continued to ignore its pronouncements and serve as clearinghouses for smuggled ivory.

Around the world, conservation organizations like the World Wildlife Fund and Wildlife Conservation International took up the elephants' cause and launched a massive public education effort. They publicized the fact that there was a cause-and-effect relationship between the purchase of ivory and the imminent extinction of elephants. The summer of 1989 was called Save the Elephant Summer.[22] Information on the plight of elephants appeared regularly in the press and on television.

At first the publicity backfired. Potential buyers, fearing the extinction of the elephants, increased their demands, causing the value of ivory to skyrocket to over $100 a pound.[23] Poaching increased! In 1989 customs officials in Tanzania, Namibia, Singapore, and Burundi stopped the shipment of thousands of tons of elephant tusks. Some had been packed in shipping crates marked "marble," "beeswax," and "jewelry." The illegal shipments would not have been attempted without the collusion of international bankers, diplomats, and government officials. The trafficking of elephant tusks earned millions of dollars.[24]

In the end, however, the publicity worked. The public heeded the warnings and boycotted ivory products. The combination of the refusal of people all over the world to purchase ivory and the enforcing of the international agreement to ban ivory by some governments has, it is hoped, saved the elephants from extinction. Although some people still buy ivory, the large market for it is gone. Unfortunately, so are most of the elephants.

While ivory poaching continues, its pace is a great deal slower. Typically the process of illegally obtained

The ivory trade was a lucrative business for many, yet the same merchants who had profited from the illegal poaching of elephants were forced to abide by the international ban on the ivory trade in 1989.

elephant tusks becoming consumer items begins when poachers hack off the entire lower jaws of elephants.[25] Sometimes poachers stockpile the jaws or the ivory in hidden places in the forest, with the intention of returning later. In the meantime they leave the rest of the carcass on the ground to rot. Sometimes poachers cover the carcasses with branches in order to delay their detection by game wardens. By the time the vultures feast on the carcasses, the poachers are gone.

After killing a number of elephants, the poachers return to their stashes and gather the tusks. The next step is to sell them to representatives of import-export companies. Many of these are Arab-owned, like the Al-Waffa Enterprises in Tanzania. The people who actually do the killing may earn as little as five dollars per pound, but each time a tusk changes hands, its price increases.

Usually hired workers load the tusks into trucks and later hide them in gas tanks, shipping crates, or personal luggage. Drivers then transport the tusks to collection points (ports such as Pangani) along the African coast. At the ports, workers mix the poached tusks with the legal ones, tons of tusks in all. Entire batches are then shipped to brokers, in places such as Dubai, a member of the United Arab Emirates. The brokers divide the tusks among carvers in the United Arab Emirates, Japan, Hong Kong, Taiwan, China, and India, who turn the tusks into consumer products. The completed articles are then exported and sold to consumers.

All this international shipping takes a great deal of paperwork. Since there is both legal and illegal ivory, it is easy for crafty people to forge documents.[26]

AFRICAN RHINOCEROSES

As the elephant population has decreased, poachers have turned to two other ivory sources. One, mentioned earlier, is the Alaskan walrus; the other is the African rhinoceros. There are two species of the African rhinoceros—the black rhinoceros and the white rhinoceros. The black rhinoceros is more frequently poached than the white rhinoceros because its horns are thicker.

In 1965 there were probably 200,000 black rhinoceroses in Africa, with the largest concentration in the Zambezi Valley in Zimbabwe.[27] While hunters had been killing rhinoceroses for centuries, serious trouble began in January 1985 (four years before Save the Elephant Summer) when the Zimbabwe officials found evidence of organized rhino poaching.[28] As time passed, the problem escalated. By 1990, experts estimated that poachers had reduced the entire African rhinoceros population to 9,000.[29] Two years later experts estimated that perhaps fewer than 2,000 black rhinoceroses remained.[30]

Today no rhinoceroses are left in Uganda, Sudan, or the Central African Republic.[31] According to Glen Tathum, the chief warden for operations in the Zimbabwe National Parks Department, "the black rhinoceros is on the brink of collapse in Africa." Tathum believes that by 1994 no black rhinos will be living outside game preserves.[32]

Like elephants' tusks, rhinoceroses' horns become decorative objects in the hands of expert carvers. However, the motivation for owning rhinoceroses' horns has a particular twist. In Yemen many young men aspire to own carved daggers made of rhinoceroses' horns, which have become a status symbol.[33] These horns can be very

(Facing page, top) Because rhino horns are prized for their ornamental value and alleged medicinal powers, poachers have decimated the rhinoceros populations in several African nations.

(Right) These rhino horns were confiscated by law enforcement authorities in Taiwan. Many Asians believe that, when ground up into a fine powder, rhino horns will enhance sexual potency.

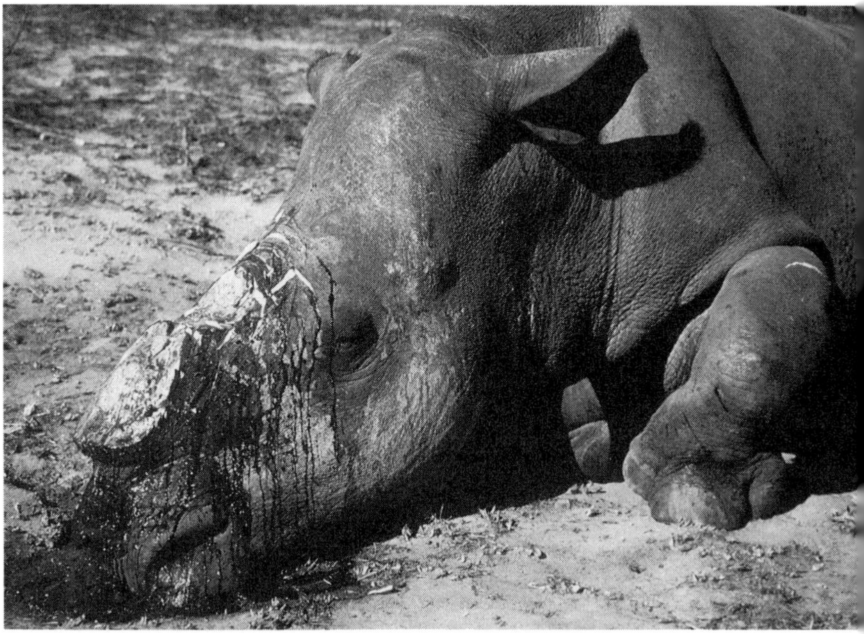

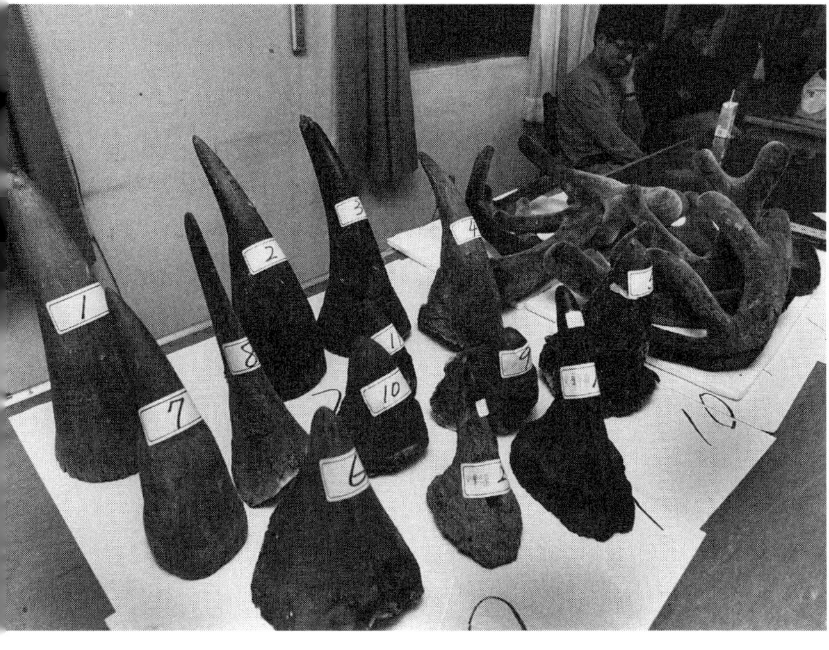
1
7
8
2
3
10
6
4
9

expensive, especially when they are embedded with precious and semiprecious stones.

In addition to this singular demand, many Asians believe that powdered rhinoceroses' horns, like powdered bears' gallbladders, have medicinal aphrodisiacal properties. As with bears' gall, there is no evidence to support this theory. Although it is illegal to import rhinoceros products into Yemen and Hong Kong, they arrive there regularly. Yemen imports three times as many rhinoceroses' horns as does any other country in the world.[34]

Rhinoceros hunters are generally African villagers. They are armed with high-powered rifles and are interested only in the horns, which they sell for twenty or thirty dollars each to entrepreneurs who smuggle them out of the country via international airports and harbors. Both the hunters and the entrepreneurs have connections with government officials and by means of bribery are able to obtain export licenses. On the documents they sometimes claim that the horns are other things. Through the years, poachers have moved from nation to nation bribing customs officials and falsifying documents in a variety of creative ways.

The illegal shipments of rhinoceroses' horns follows a winding trail from Zambia to Zaire, Malawi, Burundi, and Sudan. Most of them end up in North Yemen and the Far East.[35]

OTHER MAMMALS

Leopards, snow leopards, jaguars, tigers, gibbons, chimpanzees, orangutans, and flying squirrels are among the numerous other mammals that are still in danger of being poached. Each has its own price tag and its own smuggling route. Each is desired for its own unique reason.

Some mammals, like the primates, become exotic pets. Others die for the sake of fashion when made into clothing or rugs. Some mammals, of course, are eaten, in whole or in part. Monkey brains and eyes are Asian delicacies.[36] Tigers' bones are ingested by believers in Chinese folk medicine. Druggists who serve the Chinese communities inside and outside of China, sell these bones as a cure for rheumatic pain, rat bites, typhoid fever, dysentery, and other ailments.[37]

In 1989 there were forty-four Bengal tigers in the Ranthambhor National Park, a tiger preserve in India. The problem of tiger poaching first came to light in 1991, and has been increasing ever since. In May 1992, after an outbreak of poaching, only fifteen were left in the park.[38] It was not until the summer of 1992 that China announced a ban on the trade in tigers. Before then it was legal for factories in China to process tigers' bones poached from other countries. Officials in India estimated that poachers killed more than 100 Bengal tigers a year in order to supply their bones to factories in China.

The new law, however, did not stop poachers. In September 1993, officials in New Delhi, India, confiscated half a ton of Bengal tiger bones, 43 panther skins, and 163 skins of other animals. They estimated their value to be $650,000. The tiger bones were probably en route to mainland China.[39] A tiger yields between fifteen and fifty pounds of bones and can earn a gunner $85 to $125 per pound.[40] Its skin is worth about $1,000. The retail price for tigers' bones is about $185 per pound, but the skins can sell for as much as $30,000 each.[41] As of 1994, an estimated 5,000 Bengal tigers were left in the wild.[42]

The Amur, or Siberian, tiger is also in danger of extinction. The world's remaining population—250 to 500—live in the Sikhote-Alin Nature Reserve in Siberia. In 1992 and 1993, poachers killed 100 of them, almost one-third of the world's population. There were once eight subspecies of tigers living in Russia. Four of them—Bali, Javan, Chinese, and Caspian—are probably extinct.[43] Tigers are among the most endangered species in the world.

Orangutans aren't doing very well, either. According

Like elephants and rhinos, leopards and tigers are valued for medicinal purposes, yet their beautiful pelts also carry a deadly price tag.

to the World Wildlife Fund there are only 20,000 left—5,000 in Sumatra and 15,000 in Borneo. In 1983 there were 50,000. The giant panda is another endangered species, with only about 1,000 left in the wild.

As long as there are people willing to buy endangered animals or their parts, and as long as the penalties for illegal hunting are less certain than the rewards, poaching will continue with the inevitable result that some animal populations will continue to dwindle until there are none left.

CHAPTER 5

BIRDS: DEAD OR ALIVE

Bird poaching is a serious, widespread environmental problem. Feathered creatures, like furred ones, in every nation on earth fall to poachers' guns or nets. Although governments prohibit the shooting of certain birds, poachers shoot them anyway. These poachers have little regard for the long-term effects on the welfare of the species they kill. They bring down birds for food, sport, money, and personal adornment. Their activities may be part of large-scale, illegal businesses or the action of single individuals hunting alone or in groups.

Different bird species attract poachers for different reasons. For example, hunters may poach ducks for "fun," songbirds for pets, rare exotic birds with bright plumage for feathers, and predators for sport. They poach not only the birds, but also their eggs. The eggs may be consumed as food or hatched in incubators; the newborn birds are then sold or bred. Some poachers kill the birds, but others prefer to capture them alive. Poachers sell live birds as pets or for breeding and dead ones for food or for their parts.

In airports around the world, authorities have stopped poachers with live birds or fertile eggs sewn into their clothing or packed into their suitcases. Bird and egg poachers have become quite ingenious in finding methods of eluding officials. Sometimes the birds and eggs are smuggled across the borders in secret compartments of cars or trucks.

Whether bird poachers shoot their quarry in flight, snatch them while feeding, or rob them from nests, they ignore the laws because it is profitable to do so.

DUCKS AND OTHER WATERFOWL

Hunters kill waterfowl primarily for "fun" and secondarily for food. It is common for hunters of ducks and other waterfowl to violate game laws. In some areas of the United States, federal wildlife agents have estimated that as many as 92 percent of duck hunters poach! According to David Hall, a law enforcement agent of the United States Fish and Wildlife Service, "It looks like the guys who hunt illegally are taking four times more than the guys who hunt legally . . . [and] it's every place I've ever worked."[1]

One-quarter of all North American ducks migrate through Louisiana to the South American continent each winter. Fifty years ago this migration comprised thirty million ducks, and the supply seemed inexhaustible. Today only ten million ducks migrate annually, and this number is dropping. Duck hunting in Louisiana is a long-standing tradition. Many people who live in the bayou country believe it's their right to kill as many ducks as they please.[2] Poaching, in fact, "is a way of life."[3]

Duck poachers in general scorn the limits on the number of ducks they may kill each day, use electronic birdcalls, disregard the hunting season, and frequently fire lead shot instead of steel. Lead shot poisons thousands of birds when they ingest the lead from spent shells. They take it in as grit and die within forty-eight hours.[4]

Waterfowl poachers are often young men between

Huge flocks of migratory birds are prime targets for poachers in North America.

the ages of twenty and thirty. They are usually well-equipped hunters who belong to sports clubs and organizations like Ducks Unlimited. Ducks Unlimited is a hunting organization that spends a significant amount of money protecting the natural habitats of ducks, but it also fights to prevent legislation that would require hunters to use steel shot.[5]

Most duck poachers hunt close to their homes, know the territory well, and feel secure in their environment. They are not novices making mistakes. In fact, they are not only informed about hunting laws, but are better informed about laws regarding waterfowl than are nonviolators of these laws.[6]

Poachers do not confine themselves to their home states. Affluent people, including business executives, elected officials, and even judges, are willing to spend $65 to $500 a day on hunting trips.[7] They arrange their expeditions through hunting organizers. People who earn incomes arranging duck-hunting trips are successful if their hunters are happy, and hunters are happy when they bring down birds. To increase the opportunities to do so, some organizers use airboats that stir up the waterfowl and force them to fly toward the waiting gunners. Such unethical organizers repeatedly encourage these "sportspeople" to take more than their legal limits. They may even scatter corn or rice on the surface of the water to attract more birds, an illegal practice called baiting. In Louisiana, for example, during the duck season there is a great increase in the sale of corn and rice.[8]

When a group of hunters open fire over baited water, so many birds drop at one time that it is impossible for the hunters to retrieve them all. According to a report made by an eyewitness during a Fish and Wildlife Service sting operation in Louisiana, "Everybody kills until they run out of shells."[9] This practice, however, is not limited to Louisiana.

Thousands of birds die when they ingest poisonous lead from spent shells. The U.S. Fish and Wildlife Service now requires hunters to use steel shot.

Wherever such hunting occurs, the result is wanton waste. Although there is a legal limit to the number of waterfowl a hunter may kill in any one day, it is common for poachers to falsify records claiming some of the birds were killed by other people, including some who were not even hunting on the day that they were.[10] The limit on the number of birds a hunter may shoot depends upon the breed of the bird, the season, and the state in which the hunting takes place.

Some birds are illegal to hunt. For example, for more than seventy years it has been illegal to hunt the beautiful, yellow-crowned night heron. Nevertheless, poachers continue to stalk this bird, especially the ones that are too young to fly. In bayou country the *gros becs* (pronounced "grow becks"), as the young birds are called, are a favorite dinner entree.[11] Poachers sell them for as little as three to five dollars each.[12] In their eagerness to shoot whatever flies, poachers also bring down golden plover, belted kingfishers, killdeers, anhingas, snow geese, and blue geese—other birds that it is illegal to kill.[13]

Waterfowl poaching is not limited to Louisiana. In Texas an undercover investigation revealed an ongoing problem with illegal duck hunting in Texas.[14] Wisconsin also has a problem with duck poachers. As of this writing, the Department of Natural Resources in Madison, Wisconsin, has a walk-in freezer containing confiscated waterfowl, even a dead swan. These birds, shot by overzealous hunters, are being kept as evidence for criminal trials.

Thousands of waterfowl, including egrets, ibis, and wood storks migrate back and forth between the United States, Mexico, and South America. Despite the fact that they are protected by treaty, during migration the birds are shot on both sides of the borders.[15]

Sometimes poachers steal the eggs of waterfowl. For example, in June 1990, several Vietnamese-Americans raided pelican nests and stole eighty-three eggs. Authorities caught them before they could either sell or eat their catch. Although the wardens took the eggs to a hatchery, most of the embryos died before they hatched.[16]

BIRDS OF PREY

For centuries falconers—hunters who use birds of prey, or raptors, to help them hunt—have captured, bred, and trained these birds. Falconry was a sport that began in Asia over 4,000 years ago and continues to this day.

Many hunters choose to ignore the legal
limits placed on the number of waterfowl that
may be killed in one day. If caught, these
people face fines and imprisonment.

Among the most prized hunting birds are the peregrines, gyrfalcons, goshawks, Harris's hawks, and eagles. In the United States only licensed falconers are permitted to trap hunting birds and the laws governing their activities are very explicit. For example, falconers may trap only young birds and only those migrating for the first time.

In addition they may remove eggs or very young birds from their nests, but only during certain seasons.[17]

To obtain a license a person has to learn a great deal about hunting birds and pass a series of tests. Licensed falconers are usually ethical people and find bird snatching distasteful. They are also usually willing to work with authorities to help catch poachers.[18]

Falconers, whether licensed or not, and whether in Europe, the Middle East, or the United States, are willing to spend large sums of money for healthy raptors. Their willingness to do so encourages poaching. In Saudi Arabia falconers will pay as much as $50,000 to $100,000 per bird. Although some birds of prey are bred in Saudi Arabia, others are imported and often poached.[19]

Hunting birds are a special target for egg snatchers.[20] Eggs don't make noise and don't have to be fed. Often it is easier to remove eggs than live birds from nests. Sometimes, however, it is necessary to capture or kill the parents in order to get their eggs. Poachers do whatever is necessary to get the eggs and transport them to places where they can be hatched in incubators and later sold.

In Europe there is a lucrative black market in the feathers of eagles, owls, and hawks.[21] In 1983, for example, a feathered warbonnet sold for $5,000 and a single eagle feather for $1,000.[22]

Most of the feathers go to buyers in Japan, Germany, Great Britain, and Eastern Europe. Some Europeans and Asians collect feathers because they are interested in American history. Cowboy and Indian clubs are popular among adults outside the United States. Members of these clubs use feathers to adorn their costumes.[23]

Some Native American craftspeople use feathers to make such things as headdresses, rattles, jewelry, and lances. Other Native Americans use some of these articles in their ceremonial and religious practices and sell others to tourists. For example, some people like to hang eagles' claws, or talons, on the rearview mirrors of their

There are many licensed practitioners of falconry, a sport that dates back more than 4,000 years, yet because a healthy hunting bird can go for as much as $50,000 to $100,000, many poachers are willing to snatch the eggs of hawks and falcons and sell them on the black market.

automobiles and display feathers in decorative arrangements in their homes.[24]

The law allows certain members of some Native American tribes to take a limited number of eagles from their own reservations and use the feathers and other parts of these birds. If, however, these authorized persons can't get as many feathers as needed, the United States Fish and Wildlife Service will provide them as they become available. One problem is that not all Native Americans may get feathers in this way; only those, such as religious leaders, who are officially authorized to do so, may. To get eagle feathers from the government, the authorized persons must complete numerous legal documents. In 1990 the Fish and Wildlife Service received 1,209 requests for whole eagles, parts, and feathers but were able to fulfill only 766.[25] Thus, even when the Fish and Wildlife Service wants to supply the requested feathers, it may take as long as eighteen months for authorized people to get them. It's much easier to poach eagles. This poaching may take place on neighboring reservations, in national parks, in bird sanctuaries, or elsewhere.[26]

Native Americans, though, are not the only eagle poachers. For example, Ralph Jackson, a Caucasian from Sequim, Washington, earned half a million dollars by killing twenty-five bald eagles. He also earned twelve years in jail.[27]

In 1974, a big, illegal feather operation took place in South Dakota and Nebraska. Although the authorities apprehended and fined the culprits, they resumed their business in 1983 and were again apprehended and fined. In 1992, federal agents arrested the adult children of these eagle poachers. They had learned the business from their parents.[28]

A favorite method of poaching eagles is for gunners to shine lights into the trees where eagles roost. The lights both reveal and freeze the birds, making them easy targets.[29] In Madison, Wisconsin, in 1993, a dead eagle found in a freezer was confiscated by the Fish and Wildlife Service and held as evidence of this kind of poaching.

SONGBIRDS AND EXOTIC BIRDS

Some black marketers deal in songbirds, the hunting of which is illegal. Poachers sometimes capture songbirds

Certain Native American craftsmen are granted permission to use otherwise protected bird feathers for headdresses, rattles, or jewelry, but sometimes bird parts find their way into the wrong hands, and single eagle feathers have been sold for as much as $1,000.

alive and sell them as pets or for breeding. On occasion, however, poachers sell songbirds as food, particularly in Louisiana, Arkansas, and Mississippi. In these states, night-roosting robins are especially popular.[30]

While rare exotic birds with beautiful, unusual feathers are sold live as pets and for breeding purposes, they are also killed for their plumage.

The fascination with feathers has put birds such as scissor-tailed flycatchers, flickers, and even bluebirds and magpies in danger. A flicker hat pin can sell for ten dollars, and a scissor-tail fan is worth as much as $700.[31]

Many people around the world find colorful birds so attractive that they display them as ornaments after they have been stuffed. According to the Convention on International Trade in Endangered Species (CITES), an international trade agreement, traffic in birds of paradise is illegal. However, because of their ornamental plumage, they are particularly desirable birds—dead or alive. West German taxidermists have been known to get these birds from Indonesia or New Guinea, stuff and mount them, then sell them as up-market souvenirs to buyers throughout Southeast Asia.[32]

Since exporting these birds is illegal, poachers will go to a great deal of trouble to conceal their product. One ploy they use is to claim that the birds are of another species. To do this, a dealer may take birds of paradise and dye their plumage black, so that they look like crows. The dealer will then "legally" ship the "crows" to customers. Within a year the birds will molt, regrow their ornamental feathers, and again look like birds of paradise.[33]

Parrots also are frequently poached. Captive-bred parrots (those born to birds already in captivity) may be legally bought and sold, but those that are wild-caught may not. Nevertheless, wild-caught birds are smuggled into the United States from Mexico and sold in pet shops.[34] The dealers may or may not know the truth, and few buyers care.

It is illegal in the United States to net certain North American birds, such as the indigo bunting, lazuli bunting, and cardinal. However, during their migration period these birds fly south and are netted and sold in Mexico to Asian bird marketeers.[35] International treaties make this illegal, but the activity continues nevertheless.

Today the major exporters of wild birds are in Indonesia. Dealers there export not only their protected birds, such as the hornbill, but also protected birds from other countries. It is easy for smugglers who capture birds in Australia and New Guinea to transport them to markets in Jakarta, Indonesia, because of its location. From Indonesia they fly these birds to places such as Singapore, Malaysia, and Great Britain.[36]

The bird market in Bangkok, Thailand, is another well-known place in which to buy exotic birds. On any weekend a buyer can choose from perhaps a hundred different species, of which 90 percent have been poached.[37]

Sixty airlines, including every one in the United States, will no longer ship wild-caught birds. This makes shipping these birds by air difficult, but not impossible. A few non-U.S. airlines still allow the transportation of wild-caught birds. When air travel is unavailable, poachers use alternative means, such as boats and trucks. For example, some birds are transported in secret compartments within trucks from Bangkok to Hat Yai, Thailand, near the Malaysian border, then on to Singapore.

One can find numerous protected Thai birds in the bird markets of Singapore, including the red-whiskered bulbul and the white-eye. It is estimated that 50,000 Singapore inhabitants own caged songbirds. While it is perfectly legal to own many of these birds, it is illegal to own many others. For example, the shama is a restricted bird—that is, only a limited number of them may be caught and sold. Yet the number of them available in Singapore exceeds this quota a hundredfold.[38]

Bird-smuggling rings link many nations, including Denmark, Finland, Germany, the United Kingdom, Iceland, Saudi Arabia, and the United States, with nations in Asia, Africa, and Latin America.[39]

Any bird born in captivity can be legally traded. The problem is that too often dealers supplement their stock with wild-caught birds and simply forge the documents. It is a simple task to manipulate leg bands or add wild-caught birds to the stock of a cooperating domestic breeder. Lying comes easily to poachers. Forging documents and then selling birds on the international market is both easy and profitable.[40]

BIRD TRAPPERS

Bird trappers are highly skilled people. Since there is no point in capturing or killing birds that have no commercial value, trappers must be able to identify many different species in their adult and juvenile stages. This is often difficult, as several species may look quite similar and a young bird may not resemble an adult of the same species. Bird trappers must be able to identify birdcalls and know if a particular species lives in trees, marshlands, grassy areas, or on hilltops. They must also know the breeding habits and foods (such as insects, seeds, meat, or flower nectar) of many species of birds.

When a trapper goes to work, he or she needs to be equipped with various devices such as nets, traps, ropes, and bags, and various baits. The devices and the baits used depend upon the birds being sought. A trapper must know what works best for each bird.

Once a bird is captured, the trapper must keep it alive. Feeding a wild bird is no easy task, and many die before they reach market. Trapped birds are likely to be frightened and try to escape. The trapper must keep this from happening and at the same time prevent the bird from injuring itself. One way to keep it from getting hurt

Poachers who illegally capture birds of paradise must know not only their feeding and nesting habits, but must devise methods to protect them from harm when they are transported to market.

is to limit its movements severely. To do this the trapper has several options, including taping the bird's wings tightly to its body or stuffing the bird into a small tube. Still another way to prevent a bird from moving is to keep it in darkness. To maintain a fairly large bird in the dark, the trapper might decide to "seel" it. To seel a bird a trapper inserts a threaded needle through the bird's lower eyelid. The trapper pulls the thread over the bird's head, then through its other lower eyelid. Finally the trapper knots the thread so it won't come loose.[41]

It is not easy being a trapper, especially as the numbers of available birds keep decreasing. Professional bird trappers usually learn their skills and acquire their information from family members who are already experienced trappers. Bird trapping as a means of earning a living is often a parent-to-child occupation.[42]

CHAPTER 6

SWIMMERS, SWARMERS, AND PLANTS

Poachers do not limit their activities to the illegal collecting of land mammals and birds. On the contrary, poaching from the waterways of the world is as lucrative and as common as poaching from the land and the air. According to the World Wildlife Fund, three reptiles—hawksbill sea turtles, bog turtles, and Orinoco crocodiles—are among the ten most endangered species of the world, and part of the reason is poaching. At one time alligators were on the brink of extinction because of poaching. Although they are still being poached, they are in far less danger than they once were. Poachers also illegally harvest clams, salmon, and other water life, as well as plants and insects. Wherever people poach and whatever they harvest illegally, their motives remain the same: food, money, greed, and vanity. People who steal from land, water, or air, whether on a large scale (as the taking of tons of fish at one time) or a small scale (as the netting of a single birdwing butterfly—one of the rarest butterflies on earth) lessen the value of the world we share.

CLAMS

Clams are found in rivers, lakes, and oceans. Their meat is valued, as are their shells and the pearls that are found in some of them. Laws govern the harvesting of clams just as they do the hunting of mammals and birds. As long as they are the right species and size and are in season, clams can be taken using proper methods. Clams take a long time to grow in their natural habitats, and during some parts of the year, in certain waters, their meat can be very toxic.

Americans think of clams mainly as food, but their shells have value as well. Dealers export clam shells primarily to Japan, where workers punch bits out of the thickest parts and implant these bits into oysters. To the oyster, the shell bit is an irritant, and to deal with the irritant the oyster secretes a fluid that adheres to the clam shell bit and in time becomes a pearl. The longer the shell remains within the oyster, the larger the pearl. Clams as well as oysters grow pearls.[1]

Poachers reduce clam populations to dangerously low levels. When they work during closed seasons (April to September in many places), they limit the clams' ability to reproduce. When poachers use illegal harvesting methods, they destroy the clam beds. One illegal method involves the dredging of river bottoms with a metal contraption called a back hoe. A back hoe looks like a bucket and digs six to eight inches into the clam bed. As the hoe moves, it disrupts the entire ecosystem, including the clam beds, at the bottom of the river. Another illegal harvesting method is where the clammer walks through the water, feels for shells with his or her feet, and then digs up the clams by hand. Sometimes poachers work at night in order to avoid detection. Whether digging clams by hand or using a metal contraption, poachers regularly remove both undersized clams and endangered species of clams.[2]

Poachers often harvest clams from polluted waters, which can sicken or even kill people who eat such clams. Some clamming areas are closed seasonally because of red tides, or red blooms—seawater discolored by large invasions of plankton that produce a powerful poison when they die. The poison contaminates the water, gets into the clams, and is passed along to people who eat them. Some areas also are closed because of pollution created by humans—for example, oil spills or raw sewage, which may inadvertently end up in the ocean. Poachers may ignore such closings.

Experienced clam poachers can earn as much as $500 to $1,000 for an evening's work, particularly when they find pearls.[3] Pearlers who search for pearls open every clam they find, including endangered ones such as the perale higginseye. They discard everything but the pearls, leaving behind heaps of wasted wildlife. Clam poaching, like other poaching, is market driven. When the market price for clams or pearls goes up, so does the quantity poached.[4]

SALMON

In recent years there has been a sharp decline in the salmon population. Salmon are a species hunted both by commercial fishermen and sport anglers. Several years ago the drop in the salmon population became alarming. The decline was so great that many concerned citizens feared the extinction of the salmon.

Overfishing was only one of the causes. Hydroelectric dams (which destroy habitats), pollution, pesticides, chemicals, acid rain, and lack of enforcement of treaty rights among nations added to the problem.

In 1982, federal and state agencies blamed Native Americans in Oregon for part of the problem, but the Indians responded by saying that fishing fleets were catching too many salmon at sea and salmon hatcheries were raising too few salmon. Occasionally authorities have declared that Native Americans are largely responsible for the decline of salmon in certain areas of the Northwest. They accused the Native Americans of engaging in numerous illegal activities, including placing nets under log rafts, eavesdropping on game wardens, disabling wardens' boats, and using children to help conceal their caches of fish.[5] While some Native Americans might have been guilty of these practices, other poachers were equally to blame.

By 1983, salmon had become so desirable and scarce that poaching became a highly organized business. Salmon were selling for ten dollars a pound wholesale on the black market. The fish were said to be "too valuable to be allowed to go on living."[6] According to some authorities, the illegal take of salmon was one-third to one-half of the legal take.[7]

Soon salmon poaching became an international issue. Senator Frank Murkowski of Alaska wrote a letter to the *New York Times* on March 4, 1989, calling attention to Soviet fishers who set up nets 30 miles (48 km) long claiming to be fishing for squid, a much less valuable sea creature than salmon. In reality, these fishing nets were catching salmon. Senator Murkowski said the salmon trade was so profitable that laundering salmon money—disguising profits by moving the money through legitimate businesses—had become as sophisticated as laundering narcotics money.

Senator Murkowski pointed out that it was illegal for squid fleets to unload salmon at their home ports. To get around this, the so-called squid fishers transferred the salmon at sea to boats that took them to safe ports like Singapore or Hong Kong. From there the fish were moved directly to market, to freezing stations, or to canning centers in Bangkok or elsewhere. The eventual destinations for salmon caught in American waters were Europe and Australia.[8]

Although Native Americans and Soviet fishers received a great deal of negative publicity for poaching, they were not the only ones stealing salmon from U.S. waters. In April 1989, the U.S. government cracked an

Asian salmon-poaching ring that had netted 1.5 million pounds of salmon. Like their Soviet counterparts, Asian fishers caught salmon in nets designed to take squid. The U.S. government discovered seventeen individuals and corporations in Taipei, Hong Kong, Tokyo, and San Francisco involved in a salmon-fishing scam. The poachers shipped the salmon to the U.S. ports of Oakland, California, and Bellingham, Washington, then froze, packaged, and shipped them to Japan for sale. Together they formed a sophisticated network of front companies.[9]

Salmon poaching continues to be an international problem. In May 1990, the Soviet Union arrested 140 Japanese fishers sailing in North Korean fishing boats in the North Pacific. They had caught thousands of tons of salmon that originated in Soviet waters but were migrating to Japan. Profits were expected to be in the tens of millions of dollars, with the split to be made by Japan and North Korea. When it became apparent that there was a secret agreement between Japanese and North Korean fishing fleets, the incident became a major political embarrassment to Japan. It was a clear violation of a Soviet-Japan fishing treaty. The Soviets accused the fishing crews of "malicious poaching."[10]

OTHER FISH PROBLEMS

While the main type of fish poaching is overfishing, there are other types, too. For example, under the Lacey Act, commercial importers may not buy fish poached from waters of foreign nations. That is, if a Canadian fishing fleet catches more sturgeon in Canadian waters than Canada allows, the American importer may not purchase the excess for resale in the United States.

Another type of fish poaching is the buying and selling of endangered species. For example, the Malayan bonytongue, a tiny fish found in Indonesia and Malaysia, is protected by both the Endangered Species Act and the

Convention on International Trade in Endangered Species (CITES) and therefore may not be legally traded. Nevertheless, pet shops in the United States have been known to sell them.[11]

There is a considerable amount of poaching among sport fishers simply because there are so many of them. Sport fishers are guilty of poaching when they keep undersized fish, use more fishing lines than the law allows, have more hooks on their lines than permitted, take more fish than the law grants, or keep species for which they do not have permits. They are also guilty of poaching if they sell the fish they catch.

Sometimes sport fishers are more interested in fish eggs than in fish. For example, sturgeons' eggs are a very expensive delicacy known as caviar. In 1979 sturgeon was hard to get, so caviar producers turned to the spoonbilled paddlefish. Soon the paddlefish species became so rare that the retail price of its eggs rose to $500 a pound. The climate was perfect for poaching. A Tennessee poacher boasted that he cleared $86,000 in five nights of work. Authorities ended his poaching career in 1988.[12]

REPTILES

As with other forms of wildlife, there is a legal and an illegal market for reptiles, and the laws vary from nation to nation. Many reptiles are destined to become boots, shoes, jackets, wallets, or handbags. These fashion items are popular in Japan, Belgium, The Czech Republic, and the United Kingdom.[13] Some people buy live reptiles as high-priced toys. While hobbyists may take care of their reptiles, some casual owners quickly lose interest in them; within a year of being caught, most reptile pets die. There are also people who collect items made from reptile parts.[14] Some reptiles, especially turtles, become gourmet food.

No one knows exactly how widespread the illegal reptile trade is. Nor do wildlife officials know exactly how many reptiles are poached each year or how many of each species remain. What they do know is that almost daily they confiscate illegal shipments of reptiles. In the United States alone, although shipping reptiles through the mail is illegal, 100,000 are mailed each year.[15]

Reptiles can be found in many places, and wherever they are found they are poached. In the United States, poachers collect their crop in Arizona, Texas, New Mexico, California, Nevada, and Oklahoma and ship them by mail, car, or airplane to any places where there are buyers.[16] Poachers in Thailand catch the protected cobras, pythons, and mountain-horned agamas and sell them to collectors in Europe and Asia.[17] Alligator poachers in Paraguay, Bolivia, and Brazil do their dirty work at night. It takes only a few hours for a band of eight men to kill 200 alligators.[18]

Snakes are harder to find than alligators. Snakes lead such secretive lives that scientists find it difficult to locate some species regularly enough to study them. Poachers, however, have no difficulty rounding them up. In some places, poachers seeking snakes simply pour gasoline down hillsides to flush them out. It does not matter to them that the gasoline pollutes the water and kills turtles and other creatures that happen to be there. Some snake poachers use jackhammers, crowbars, and dynamite to widen crevices in hillsides in their efforts to find what they are looking for.[19]

The black-market price for a twin-spotted rattlesnake or desert massasauga (a ground rattlesnake) is several hundred dollars, and the rare Gila monster, a native of Arizona, sells for more than $1,000 in Japan and Europe. California is a big reptile market, as well.[20]

Turtles are another frequently poached reptile. One species, the bog turtle, has become so rare that it is a

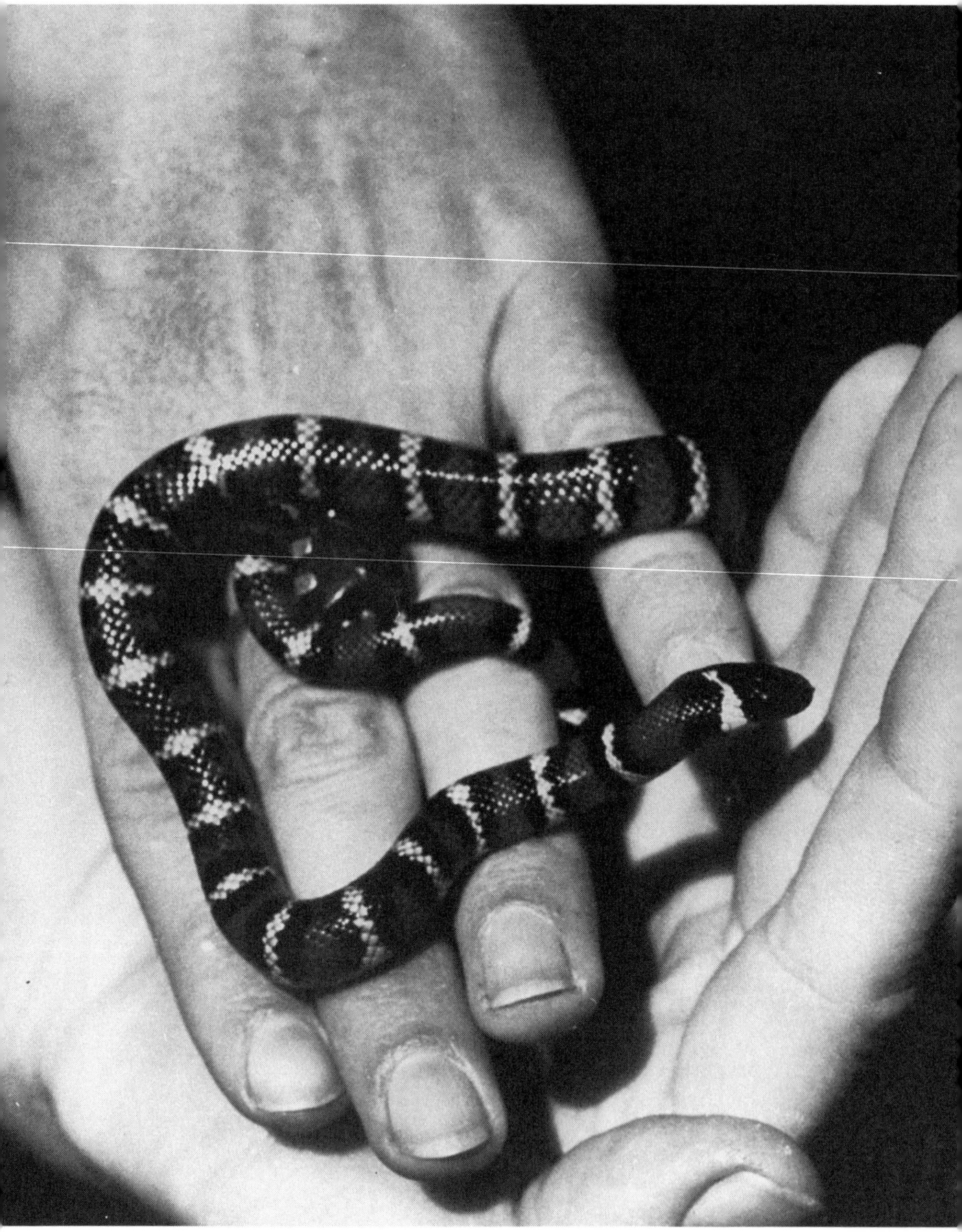

collector's item. Hobbyists are willing to pay $250 for a single male or $850 for a breeding pair. The hawksbill sea turtle is another vulnerable reptile. Even though most nations ban trade in hawksbills, poachers still catch them. People like to own tortoiseshell jewelry, hair ornaments, and furniture. The skin of the hawksbill is used to make boots, wallets, purses, and eyeglass cases. The green turtle, still another species, is an ingredient in some soups, suntan lotions, and makeup.[21]

In some places people eat sea-turtle eggs as a substitute for chicken eggs. These eggs are about the size of a chicken egg, and the turtles lay about 60 to 100 of them at one time. In 1988 sea-turtle eggs were sold for two dollars each, but as the supply went down, the price went up.[22] Today a single sea-turtle egg will sell for as much as five dollars. Sea-turtle eggs can be found in the Caribbean, where tourists dine on them in posh restaurants.[23]

PLANTS

Plant poaching is yet another widespread and serious wildlife crime. Loggers who fell trees outside their legal areas or in closed areas are poachers. People who cut Christmas trees from state or federal lands, and those who dig up ginseng plants, cacti, Venus's-flytraps, pink lady's slippers, and trilliums are poachers. Hobbyists who steal orchids and bonsai trees from one another or from public displays, and entrepreneurs who remove the bark of the rare yew trees, also are poachers.

Some pet owners and hobbyists are willing to pay several hundred dollars for rare reptiles, such as this California mountain king snake.

Ginseng is a root revered by Asians and others as a cure-all. As a legally cultivated crop, ginseng is exported to Japan from the United States in large quantities. One reason ginseng is so expensive is that the root takes up to twelve years to mature. The wholesale price is about $200 a pound, high enough to make the plant of interest to poachers.[24]

Ginseng grows wild in the upper Midwest and in its wild form is worth even more than it is in its cultivated form, especially if its twisted root has the shape of a natural object or of a human being.[25] Conservationists worry that soon there will no longer be any wild ginseng.[26]

Poachers also steal cacti. One of their favorite species is the peyote cactus, which contains mescaline, a hallucinogen used in religious ceremonies by some Native Americans. Peyote grows wild in national and state parks in the warm, dry climates of Texas and northern Mexico.[27]

Still another frequently poached plant is the saguaro cactus. The saguaro is difficult to cultivate, grows very slowly—only 1 inch (2.5 cm) a year—and reproduces only when it is at least fifty years old. One ancient saguaro cactus was a living monument of its kind in Quartzsite, Arizona, until a poacher dug it up and sold it to a nursery in Las Vegas for $15,000.

The trade in desert plants is a serious problem in the Southwest. In an effort to conserve water, state and local officials in Arizona, New Mexico, Texas, and southern California have encouraged homeowners to use desert plants for landscaping. The plan backfired when residents began poaching these plants. Some homeowners simply went into the desert and dug up what they wanted for themselves. Others dug up more than they needed and sold them to nurseries and homeowners. In a four-year period ending in 1990, poachers stole $80,000 worth of saguaro from federal and state lands.[28] As cacti became more difficult to find, people started im-

Ginseng root, seen by many as a cure-all, can take up to twelve years to mature. Because its wild form is so rare, its wholesale price has soared to $200 a pound, making it very attractive to plant poachers.

porting them illegally from Mexico. In addition, commercial operators smuggle some of the cacti to Japan, earning profits of thousands of dollars.[29]

Among the most determined plant poachers are those who hunt Venus's-flytraps. Venus's-flytrap poachers encounter ticks, snakes, and other hazards yet are willing to endure such poor working conditions because they can earn as much as $200 a day. While there is a high demand for Venus's-flytraps in Holland and Japan, most of these plants go to pharmaceutical companies in Germany. There the chemists extract from them an enzyme reputedly useful in treating cancer and AIDS.

As the habitats of the Venus's-flytrap disappear, the demand for these plants increases. Venus's-flytraps grow in only eleven counties in North and South Carolina, but there was a time when they could be found growing wild throughout both states.[30] Poachers have stolen so many Venus's-flytraps that fines for poaching them have increased from $100 to $500 per plant for the first offense and $1,000 for the second offense.

People once considered the Pacific yew tree to be a weed. After it became rare, scientists discovered that its bark contains taxol, a chemical that is expected to be used in the future as a cancer-fighting drug, but there is not a great deal of it and it is not yet available on the general market. In May 1991, poachers stripped the bark from fifty-six yew trees in Oregon's Willamette National Forest. No one seems to know what happened to the bark. It takes decades before a yew tree is mature enough for taxol to be extracted.[31]

Poachers cut down Christmas trees from beside state highways and in open areas where they grow full and straight.[32] In the winter of 1991, in an effort to stop Christmas-tree poaching, workers of the New Jersey Highway Department sprayed Christmas trees in Warren Township with a harmless substance made from bone marrow. In the cold the spray is odorless. However, according to Barbara Richardson, spokesperson for the New Jersey Transportation Department, once one of these trees is in a warm place, like someone's living room, "The meal begins to emit a stench that lingers for days even after the tree is removed. . . . It is lip-curling, a nose-wrinkling, stomach-turning smell." Christmas-tree poaching stopped quickly there. Now law enforcement agents have only to post signs warning people that they have sprayed the trees.[33] Of course, an unsuspecting buyer looking for a bargain tree might innocently purchase a sprayed one. Doing business with a legitimate dealer lessens the risk considerably.

Most dealers in plants, fish, reptiles, and other water life are honest. They care about the natural environment and do not harvest or sell what is forbidden.

CHAPTER 7

THE EFFECTS OF POACHING

Wildlife theft has consequences for all who share the earth. Poaching precipitates the extinction of species, inflicts pain and suffering and causes death to animals, promotes organized crime, damages the ecosystem, and encourages antihunting attitudes. Those who exploit wildlife are exploiting the future.

THE EFFECTS OF POACHING ON ANIMALS

Many plant and animal species are already extinct or doomed to extinction. The seemingly infinite variety of birds, mammals, reptiles, and plants that once populated this planet has diminished. Sixty million buffalo once roamed the North American continent, but their vast herds are long gone. In the 1890s the flights of billions of passenger pigeons could blacken the skies, but in 1914 the last one died in captivity.[1] There are no longer dodo birds, pie ducks, or hundreds of other species that once walked on or flew above the earth. These creatures disappeared as a result of several factors, including habitat reduction, overhunting, poor land management, and poaching.

While numerous creatures have come and gone, according to Dave Foreman, a founder of Earth First!, an environmental activist group, there has never been "such a high rate of extinction as we are now witnessing."[2] The puffins, Eskimo curlews, swifts, and sun bears are almost gone. Tigers, rhinos, and elephants are in danger. So are bobcats, jaguars, and gorillas. Governments have enough information to increase by thousands the number of species that need protection from the forces that threaten their continued existence. While politicians, conservationists, and special-interest groups argue about which species to classify as threatened or endangered, the number of imperiled species grows.

According to William K. Reilly, president of the World Wildlife Fund, poaching is the greatest threat to many of these species. For example, in 1988, in their eagerness to obtain bears' gallbladders, a group of 203 poachers in China killed 145 giant pandas, one-seventh of the world's giant panda population.[3] Six of the eight known bear species (sun bears, Asiatic black bears, grizzlies, sloths, giant pandas, and speckled bears) are in worse condition now than they were in 1970.[4] Undercover agents from Great Smoky Mountains National Park have documented the loss of 366 bears over a three-year period.[5] In 1989 the National Audubon Society estimated that only 400 to 600 bears remained in Great Smoky Mountains National Park. There are no more grizzlies in California or the southern Rocky Mountains, and only about 1,000 remain in the northern Rocky Mountains.

Poaching also has ravaged the duck population. Years ago there were 90 million ducks in the United States; in the 1990s there are fewer than 60 million. In Louisiana, where up to one-quarter of all American ducks spend the winter, the illegal take is estimated at four times the number of ducks shot legally. Poaching is reducing not only the duck population but also the populations of eagles and other migratory birds.[6]

Poaching as a threat to the continuation of species is longstanding. In Africa the slaughter of orangutans, elephants, and rhinos threatens their ability to survive. According to the World Wildlife Fund, in 1983, 50,000 orangutans were left in the world; today there are only 20,000. For a while poachers were killing elephants at the rate of three a day. Biologists warn that the number of animals killed every year is two or three times the rate at which they can reproduce.[7] In 1979 the total elephant population of Africa was estimated at 1.3 million; today it is less than half that number.

While greed motivates some hunters, and the quest for status motivates others, the consequences are the same: extinction, near extinction, or serious weakening of species. The frantic competition for record-book trophies obtained by collecting the horns and heads of animals has had an insidious effect upon various species. Wildlife agents like Joel Scrafford warn that trophy hunters rob the gene pools of the biggest and healthiest of breeds. Scrafford says that if killers continue to take the "biggest and best," soon only the mediocre will remain.[8] For instance, the older a Dall sheep is, the larger its rack. Few Dall sheep more than eight years old remain. As the number of trophy-sized Dall sheep diminishes, the problem accelerates. Scrafford warns that we now are at the point where "more and more people are competing for trophies out of fear that they'd better get them now or there won't be any left. . . . Trophy-sized animals have become so rare in the wild that people are hitting the parks hard. . . ."[9]

The black rhinoceros is another animal that is quickly disappearing. In 1960 there were 65,000 black rhinos in Africa. Twenty years later only 4,000 remained and of these, 100 lived in Zambia. Today, according to the African Wildlife Foundation, fewer than 3,100 black rhinos remain in the wild.

In April 1989, conservation groups in Namibia were so desperate that they began an experimental program to thwart horn poachers. This program, Operation Bicornis, was so named because rhinoceroses have two horns. (Bicornis means two horns.) They hoped that by remov-

It is estimated that 60 million buffalo once inhabited the North American continent, but because of the disastrous effects of poaching, there are very few that remain today.

ing the rhinos' horns before the poachers did, they would reduce the incentive to kill these animals.

To accomplish this goal, rangers began using helicopters to search for these large mammals. When they found one, they tranquilized it from the air with a medicated dart. The ground crew waited until the beast staggered and fell, and then two men sliced off its horns. A waiting veterinarian smeared the stumps with an antiseptic called Stockholm tar. The procedure is painless, and since the horns are actually hair, they grow back. The question remains as to whether these beasts will survive without their horns.[10]

Extinction of a species is only one way in which poaching affects animals. Pain is another. Animal rights groups worry that poached animals are mistreated and made to suffer needlessly. For instance, wounded birds and animals that have been shot but not retrieved are left to die a slow and painful death. In addition, young animals may die of starvation when their parents have been killed.

Many animals, including elephants and primates, live in large social groups. When poachers kill the older adults, they disrupt the entire social setting and behavior patterns of the remaining group. The young animals are unable to grow up properly and learn what they need to in order to survive.

Even animals that poachers kill outright often suffer needlessly. For instance, in Australia, Marian Gitlin Newman, president of the Kangaroo Protection Foundation, reports that although the kangaroo is listed as an endangered species, there is a huge, illegal slaughter of this animal. When the joeys (baby kangaroos) get in the way of poachers, the poachers kill them by bashing or stomping on them with their boots.[11]

Poachers who capture live animals often mistreat their prey. In Thailand, poachers regularly sneak gibbons out of the forest. They take so little care of them that not only are these primates injured en route, but many more suffocate or freeze before they even reach their destinations. Those that do arrive safely are often mistreated. Dealers in poached monkeys frequently will extract their teeth with pliers or cut them with clippers in order to make these primates harmless and hence easier to sell as house pets. However, a toothless animal has difficulty eating. In the end twenty die for each one sold.[12] People have been known to break the backs of monkeys in order to keep them docile.[13]

By the time government officials rescue animals from smugglers, these animals are frequently in bad condition. The average law-enforcment agent frequently does not know what to do with confiscated live, wild animals, especially those far from their natural habitats. In order to save these creatures, private citizens sometimes take action. For instance, two British women, Leonie Vejjajiva and Margaret Himathongkom, started a private menagerie in Thailand where they are residents, in order to care for endangered species.[14] While their efforts help, they are not enough.

THE EFFECTS OF POACHING ON HUMANS

Wildlife crime has an impact on humans as well as on animals. Law enforcement officers, poachers, and innocent people die when poaching is rampant. Some law enforcement agents say that wildlife law enforcement assignments are more dangerous than those of other types of law enforcement because most of the offenders have weapons. The poachers' willingness and ability to use these weapons place game wardens in great danger. In addition, poachers are often better equipped than law enforcement officials.[15]

Poachers also are in danger of losing their own lives. In Kenya, for example, poachers are shot on sight.[16] If a park ranger makes an incorrect evaluation, an innocent person may die. However, if rangers don't shoot first and ask questions later, they place their own lives in danger. Poachers do not hesitate to shoot people who try to interfere with their activities. They have even killed tourists unfortunate enough to get in their paths or foolish enough to attempt to photograph them.[17]

Poachers kill people indirectly, as well. For example, when profiteers remove large quantities of fish from polluted waters and sell them to fish vendors, they threaten public health. People can become quite sick, even die, by eating fish that comes from unsafe waters. When the quantity of fish that has been obtained by poaching is large and the motive is profit, poachers usually will find ways to sell their contaminated catch to fish dealers who supply markets and restaurants.[18] Finding the origins of a particular fish is impossible except by chemical analysis. The danger is real enough so that many people avoid eating fish entirely.[19]

Another effect of poaching on humans is an increase in organized crime. Each year poachers take millions of tropical fish, wild birds, turtles, lizards, snakes, and other reptiles as well as the hides of fur-bearing animals. Poaching is a billion-dollar-a-year, international "industry." The illegal activity is no longer limited to killing animals for food, fun, money, trophies, personal use, or even by mistake. Instead, it has become professional, organized crime on a global scale.

In some areas of the world, poaching, like the trade in illegal drugs, is so profitable that law enforcement officers hired to protect the wildlife are part of the problem and share in the profits.[20] Legal loopholes and corruption make this trafficking hard to stop. Thailand and Indonesia are centers for the world's illegal wildlife trade.[21] Although both nations are signers of the Convention on International Trade in Endangered Species (CITES) agreement, they do little to enforce its regulations. These two countries are at the heart of the illicit trade in endangered animal such as orangutans from Asia, crocodiles from South America, rhinoceroses from Africa, and birds from Australia and New Guinea. Buyers are from all over the world.

THE EFFECTS OF POACHING ON NONHUNTERS' ATTITUDES TOWARD HUNTING

Poaching has affected the public's attitude toward hunting. When the public reads about hunters who chase animals with airplanes or airboats, when they learn how

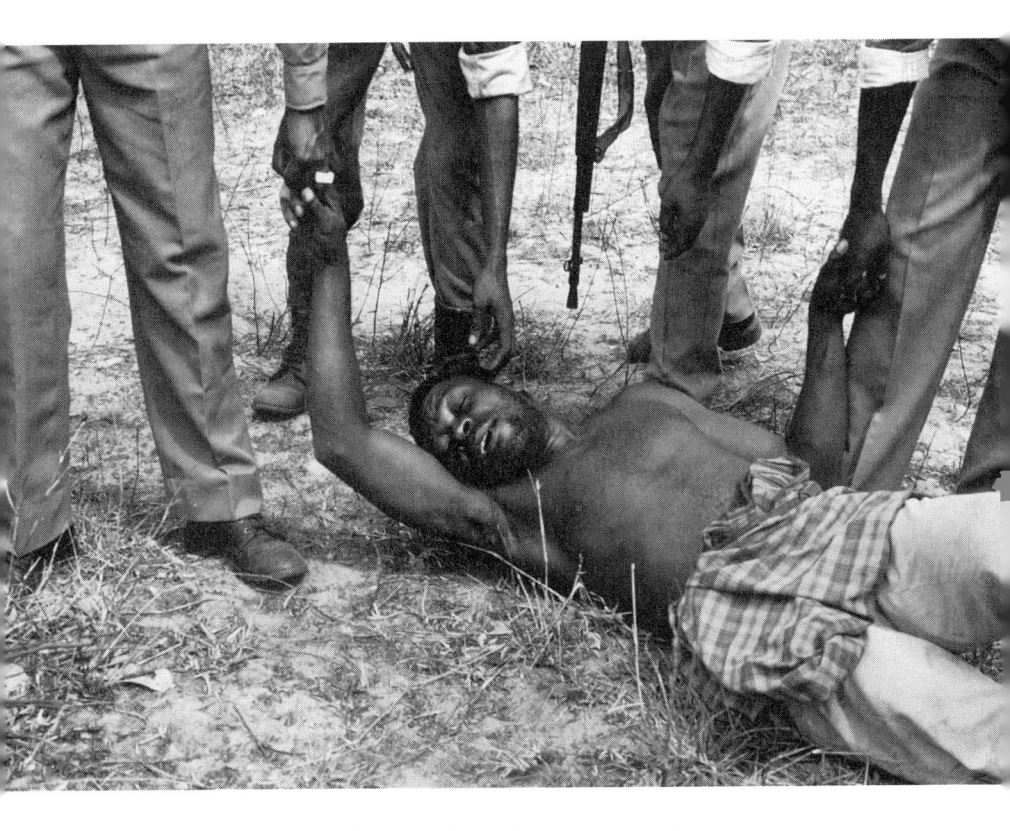

Because poachers are heavily armed and are willing to use force if necessary, game wardens put themselves at great risk in apprehending them.

hunters massacre ducks for "fun," or when they discover the widespread disregard of bag limits, nonhunters get angry at all hunters, including sport hunters. Opposition to blood sports increases each time reports call attention to poachers stalking endangered species or leaving crippled animals to die a lingering, painful death. Opposition increases further each time the public learns that poachers have killed animals in preserves and still further when they hear how much money poachers make from their illegal activities.

In order to hunt legally, a person must purchase a license. The money collected for these licenses contributes to wildlife management and the protection and preservation of the environment. Nevertheless, many nonhunters think of hunters as enemies of the environment, especially when they hear about poaching, either large- or small-scale, and regardless of whether greed, stupidity, and/or ignorance are to blame. For instance, according to Dick Brame, a wildlife coordinator for the North Carolina Wildlife Federation, not only do most duck hunters misidentify ducks in the air, but 70 percent of all duck hunters cannot identify ducks close up, including endangered species, which they sometimes shoot. This ignorance leads to wasteful death and, in turn, resentment even by tolerant nonhunters.

Many nonhunters resent the necessity of posting NO HUNTING signs on their property. The expense of making the signs and the bother of putting them on trees irritates them. The opposition to hunters in general increases every time a poacher ignores their signs and trespasses on their land.

THE EFFECTS OF POACHING ON THE ECOSYSTEM

Scientists have proven that there is an interdependent relationship between people, animals, plants, water, land, and air. Poaching irrevocably disturbs this relationship. Poaching willfully leads to the extinction of species and is a danger the far-reaching effects of which we cannot even predict. Many scientists worry that if governments allow poachers to continue to misuse and abuse the environment, future generations will pay the consequences.

Although there are some people who enjoy owning

birds of paradise, eating monkey brains, or owning tiger-skin rugs, many others believe that human beings do not have the moral right to these pleasures. Ecologists, scientists, and conservationists worry that the longer nations fail to stop poaching, the more forms of life will disappear. Once a species is gone, it is gone forever.

CHAPTER 8

CITIZENS AGAINST POACHING

Poaching sport hunters, as distinct from hard-core poachers (the criminal element or the incorrigible) fall into two categories: the weekend poacher and the big-game hunter. The former can't resist one more deer or be satisfied with the daily limit on duck or fish or whatever the quarry. The latter are willing to spend large sums of money for the thrill or honor of shooting a particular animal, even if the kill threatens the species' existence. Together they form a large group of people who pose a threat to the environment. Poachers may not think about, care about, or believe that their action could mean the permanent disappearance of an entire species. In the case of the weekend hunter in particular, the problems of extinction may seem just too far away. Game wardens insist, however, that sport hunters who poach are a bigger threat to wildlife than the hard-core professional poachers simply because there are so many more sport hunters.[1]

Realistically, poaching is probably impossible to stop entirely. Criminal poachers and poaching sport hunters will continue killing and species will continue to disappear. The situation, however, is not entirely bleak. The public can help. Wildlife crime would be worse if it were not for citizen involvement. Already public action has helped reduce poaching and perhaps even saved species that would otherwise have been doomed. While Save the Elephant Summer was probably the most dramatic example of citizen involvement, other, less publicized ways help, too.

The first step is to keep informed about the problem. Education, followed by public action, does make a difference. Only an educated public will refuse to buy unlawful wildlife products. Wildlife crime can be reduced further if people report poachers to authorities. Another way the public can help reduce poaching is by making voluntary contributions to organizations that work to protect the environment. Finally, the public can influence lawmakers by writing letters to them, expressing concern about environmental and conservation issues.

HOT LINES

The average citizen prefers not to get involved in someone else's activities. In an effort to learn more about how people react when they see wildlife crimes, the New Mexico Department of Game and Fish secretly hired a hunter to "poach" in areas where passing motorists, tourists, and local residents would be sure to see him. The department wanted to know if people reported poachers.

The undercover agent documented forty-three times that citizens saw him poaching. He killed animals that it was illegal to kill because of their ages (fawns, for instance), because of the season, or because they were in areas forbidden to hunters. Yet only once did someone inform the authorities.[2]

In order to encourage people to report wildlife crime, the New Mexico Department of Game and Fish established a hot line. The results were favorable. Hot lines were a new idea in the 1970s, but today most states have them. Antipoaching hot lines are given various

JANUARY
IVORY
CLEARANCE
SALE

names, such as TIP (Turn in Poachers), RAP (Report All Poachers), Operation Game Thief, and Game Watch. Although the ways in which hot lines work differ somewhat from one another, most function as follows:

A person wishing to report a poacher simply calls a toll-free number. Many of these numbers operate twenty-four hours a day; others can be reached only during normal business hours. The operator taking the call asks for details such as the nature of the offense and when and where it occurred. He or she asks the informant if the poacher used a vehicle, and if so, its make, model, and year. The operator also asks for a detailed description of the poacher, including hair and eye color, distinguishing marks, and clothing. It helps if the informant can also provide the poacher's name and address. It is interesting that often the informant will know the poacher personally.

State hot lines usually allow the informant to remain anonymous and sometimes offer a cash reward. These rewards range from $100 to $2,000 and come from private organizations, not public funds. Some law enforcement officers say that the anonymity rather than the reward money makes the program work. "If people had to give their names, I don't think we'd get as many calls as we do," said Larry Bell, coordinator of Operation Game Thief of the New Mexico Department of Game and Fish.[3] Others believe that without the reward money, the hot

In protest over the British and Chinese governments' rejection of the international ban on the ivory trade, French activists, dressed as elephants, set fire to ivory products outside the British embassy in Paris.

line programs would not be as successful as they are. According to Dean Tresch, a U.S. Fish and Wildlife Service special agent, "The reward is crucial to the prosecution."[4]

The Florida program has paid out nearly $140,000 in reward money since 1979. Yet 40 to 50 percent of eligible recipients turn the reward money down.[5] In Minnesota, for example, 60 percent of the hot line callers choose not to collect their rewards. Of the remaining 40 percent, some accept wildlife art prints instead. Others choose to accept the cash but then may contribute it to their favorite conservation efforts.[6]

Citizens have various reasons for reporting wildlife crimes. Some do it simply to be good citizens. They feel it's the right thing to do. Others have different motives. For example, in order to express resentment, jilted girlfriends, boyfriends, or former spouses may use these hot lines to provide information on the poaching activities of their former companions. The jilted ones take pleasure in seeing their exes in trouble. Sometimes the motive for reporting a poacher may have begun with a personal quarrel that grew into a vendetta. In order to get even, one party reports the poaching activities of the other. Sometimes disgusted hunters use hot lines to report the unethical poaching activities of hunting buddies.

According to some experts, the number of wildlife violators caught is only 2 percent. They blame this low figure on the insufficient number of conservation officers to patrol vast land areas. Having hot lines increases the number of eyes and ears available to monitor the environment. Officials in most states call the hot lines an effective and valuable deterrent. If nothing else, they scare poachers into believing the chances of getting caught are high.

In order to make it easy for a citizen to report a poacher, the National Antipoaching Foundation, at 2860

S. Circle Drive, Suite 2136, Colorado Springs, Colorado 80906, has established a nationwide hot line. A single call to 1–800–800-WARDEN will connect an individual to the proper law enforcement agency of any state in the country. The foundation pays for the cost of the phone call.

DIRECT INVOLVEMENT

While the public's use of anonymous hot lines is a great service to law enforcement efforts, other reporting methods serve as well. For example, it helps when people report suspicious happenings and unusual situations. For instance, authorities would never have caught a Wisconsin deer poacher if a gas-station employee had not reported something suspicious about a customer's automobile.

A car pulled into a gas station one Sunday evening. The driver bought gasoline, but just after he left, the attendant noticed blood on the pavement. Thinking that the driver might have a dead body in his trunk, he called the police. Law enforcement authorities stopped the vehicle on the highway, opened the trunk, and found a deer, illegally shot.[7]

In a different situation, a citizen's complaint about a neighbor led a wildlife agent to a Wisconsin farmhouse where a family was keeping a deer as a family pet. The agent reported that the animal not only was well trained, but was able to eat tortilla chips off the coffee table. The family was surprised to learn that taking a wild animal from its natural habitat was illegal and that keeping it as a pet was a form of poaching.[8]

Game wardens are usually quite happy to respond to public complaints because they frequently lead to arrests. In the fall of 1992, the Illinois Department of Conservation began receiving public complaints about hunters shooting geese. Upon investigation, agents found that forty members of nine southern Illinois goose-hunting clubs were regularly poaching geese. The individuals were cited for waterfowl violations and given fines totaling over $8,000.[9] Without these public complaints, the department might not have become aware of these poachers.

ORGANIZATIONS

On July 22, 1991, a federal court fined Michael Droptiny $4,000 and sentenced him to three years' probation, during which time he was not permitted to hunt, fish, or trap. He also was required to perform 150 hours of community service. The conviction came as a result of the information provided by an anonymous informant. The National Audubon Society rewarded this informant with $3,500. That money came from a fund founded in 1982 to help end grizzly-bear poaching. Money from that fund has led to the prosecutions and convictions of bear poachers in six out of eight cases.

The National Audubon Society is just one of many organizations dedicated to preserving animals, plants, and the other components of the natural environment. Another is the World Wildlife Fund. This association began in 1961 and has grown to be one of the most important international conservation organizations in the world. Among its numerous, specialized branches is Trade Records Analysis of Flora and Fauna In Commerce, a department known as TRAFFIC. One of TRAFFIC's aims is to curb the illegal trade in rare species of mammals, fish, birds, insects, reptiles, and plants. TRAFFIC also helps to train and equip rangers, guards, and antipoaching teams.

The Izaak Walton League of America is yet another organization committed to preserving and protecting natural resources. Founded in 1922 as a national conservation organization, today the League is committed to

When international environmental organizations called for trade sanctions against Taiwan for its refusal to ban the trade of illegal wildlife products, the Taiwanese government responded by seizing and burning more than 150 pounds (70 kg) of rhino horns, bear paws, tiger skins, and other poached items.

protecting wildlife from poachers, pesticides, loss of habitat, and water pollution.

Sometimes two organizations work together with the U.S. Fish and Wildlife Service toward a common goal. For example, in 1991 the U.S. Fish and Wildlife Service was having a great deal of difficulty stopping bird poaching in the Atchafalaya Basin of Louisiana. It needed money to hire more agents to patrol the area. Special Agent Frank Simms went to the Izaak Walton League and asked for help. The league responded with a gift of $5,000 and then asked the National Fish and Wildlife Foundation to match it. The total gift of $10,000 helped enable the U.S. Fish and Wildlife Service to hire enough agents to patrol the area daily. In this way they prevented the shooting of thousands of endangered birds by poachers.[10]

Some nonprofit organizations, however, are not what they appear to be. They may, for example, work harder to gain favorable publicity and promote hunting opportunities than they do to conserve wildlife.[11]

EDUCATION

Nonprofit conservation groups and law enforcement agencies sometimes work together to educate the public about hunting. As wildlife educators, they communicate through newspaper articles, radio programs, and television interviews. Law enforcement officers in particular concern themselves with educating the public about hunting and gun safety. They visit schools and talk about hunting ethics and the proper ways to hunt safely and legally. In addition they frequently offer classes on the subject to both adults and children. In many states people *must* take hunting-and-safety-education classes before getting a hunting license.

Wildlife educators inform hunters as to the animals and plants they are permitted and those they are forbidden to hunt. They also provide information on the personal and environmental consequences of breaking the law. While education cannot solve all our problems, it can help a great deal.

THE FUTURE

Right now, poachers are snaring, trapping, netting, and shooting thousands of rare animals and trading them on the black market. This illegal slaughter will continue as long as society rewards poachers with money or status. Poachers take beauty and leave waste. These offenders are partly responsible for an irreversible loss that deprives future generations of medical, agricultural, industrial, recreational, and spiritual wealth. The situation, however, is not entirely hopeless, for while we cannot totally eliminate wildlife crime, we can lessen its volume.

Public awareness and action has slowed the killing of elephants. The market for ivory, while not completely obliterated, has greatly diminished. Perhaps the elephant will survive. There is reason for optimism when conservation organizations and individuals such as Iain and Oria Douglas-Hamilton, Richard E. Leakey, and Daniel Moi work to raise international consciousness of the plight of various animal species.

There is hope when the governments of many nations work together to rejuvenate species and prevent their extinction. The eagle, the alligator, and the falcon were once endangered, but no longer are. There is reason to believe that conditions for tigers, rhinoceroses, elks, and bears will improve. Artist Bill Pease, a Crow Indian living on a Crow reservation in Montana, has figured out a way to make look-alike bear claws and teeth, and elk antlers and skulls from plastic resin. A Japanese pharmaceutical firm is working on a synthetic substitute for bears' gall.

There is still more reason for hope when hunters obey game laws and demand that the killings made by their hunting partners be strictly legal. There is a great deal of hope when individuals report violations and keep informed about the environment. As long as there are people who care enough to lobby for wildlife abuses to be treated as serious offenses, there is hope. The future of many wildlife species is not doomed as long as members of the international community work together in an effort to preserve the environment. Finally, there is hope if we each say "I will not be a part of the waste."

CHAPTER

PINCHERS AND POACHERS

It is often very difficult to apprehend wildlife criminals. There are not enough wardens and rangers to patrol extremely large areas of wilderness, or inspectors to monitor airports, shipping docks, and borders. One official may be responsible for more than a million acres of land.[1] In an attempt to even the odds, state governments as well as the U.S. Fish and Wildlife Service (sometimes called the FBI of the wildlife world) rely on a variety of enforcement methods, including animal forensics, decoys, dogs, and sting operations. Today government agents are assertive and sophisticated in their pursuit of poachers.

THE WILDLIFE FORENSICS LABORATORY

Probably the most helpful resource in solving wildlife crime has been the U.S. Wildlife Forensics Laboratory in Ashland, Oregon. The facility was established in 1989 at a cost of $3.5 million. At the Ashland laboratory scientists are able to determine not only that a crime has been committed but also who committed it and where it was committed.

Using a method similar to human DNA fingerprinting, the laboratory is able to match blood and tissue samples to connect specific animals to specific crimes. By running tests on the bloodstains on a hunter's clothing an investigator can determine that the animal killed was not, say, a bear that it was legal to shoot as the poacher claimed, but a protected bobcat instead.

Tests at the Ashland laboratory can determine whether the contents of unmarked bottles of liquid contain unlawful bear bile, turtle oil, or potions made from rhinoceros or elk horn. The laboratory workers also can determine the source of a minute specimen. For example, tests can determine that a small piece of flesh or fur came from a bear that had lived in Great Smoky Mountains National Park, not from the specific bear whose head is mounted on a hunter's wall.

As a result of work being done in Ashland, it is no longer as easy as it once was for poachers to get away with putting arrows into bullet holes or disguising the sex of an animal in order to claim it as a legal kill.

During an investigation, law enforcement agents around the country can send samples of confiscated animal parts to Ashland for identification. Using modern technology, scientists can now determine such things as whether a shipment of handbags is made from crocodile or alligator skins and whether the makers of the handbags obtained the skins legally or illegally. Tests on ivory objects can determine whether they were made from permissible or prohibited elephant tusks, or from the teeth of a hippopotamus, another protected animal.[2]

Through chemical analysis and the use of electron microscopes, scientists can examine the soil from an animal's feet and determine its home turf. They also can ascertain the climate in which the animal lived and the plants it ate. This information allows law enforcement agents to prove that an animal was poached from an area forbidden to hunters.

One of the successful sleuthing operations of the laboratory began as a result of the 1981 ban on importing

At the U.S. Wildlife Forensics Laboratory in Ashland, Oregon, experts are able to link animals to hunters to determine whether or not illegal poaching took place.

African elephant ivory. Despite the ban, this ivory kept arriving. Importers claimed that their tusks came from mammoths (extinct ancestors of the elephants) and that they had been legally excavated from Siberia and Alaska. No one could prove otherwise until scientists at Ashland studied the tusks under an electron microscope (an instrument capable of magnifying things thousands of times). While looking at over 10,000 tusks they found minute lines below their surfaces and realized that these lines formed one pattern in mammoths and another in African elephants. In this way they were able to prove that the suspects had committed a crime.[3]

In 1990, law enforcement agents in New Mexico suspected that a ring of elk thieves was taking live elks from public land and shipping them to a business in Canada that processed elk horns, but the authorities could not prove that these animals were being taken illegally. Ashland criminologists worked on the problem and provided the authorities with a harmless powder to spread on hay left for animals on public land. The altered feed caused the elks' urine to glow under ultraviolet light. When the poachers attempted to send more elk to Canada, officials seized these elk and examined their urine. It glowed, and the result was twenty indictments. The case became known as the Pee Glow Elk case.[4]

DECOYS AND DOGS

It many states it is illegal to travel in an automobile with a loaded gun or to shoot at animals from a moving vehicle. The latter is called roadhunting and is very dangerous; such an act can result in the death or serious injury of the hunter, the hunter's companion(s), or even innocent bystanders. The typical violator is an unsuccessful hunter who is headed home. This person may see an animal on the side of an interstate highway, and, believing it to be the last opportunity to kill for that day, shoots it. Poaching by roadhunting is common during hunting season.

Many state departments of natural resources set traps to catch roadhunters. Taxidermists make decoys from confiscated animals, which often look as though they are still alive. Game wardens then place the stuffed deer, grouse, or other animal decoys along roadsides, hide, and wait. Hunters spot the decoys and, believing them to be alive, shoot them. The waiting officers record the shots with video cameras. When the hunters try to collect their kills, or get out of their cars curious to see why the animals didn't fall down or run away, the waiting officers hand the surprised hunters citations to appear in court and pay fines. States that use this procedure have reduced roadhunting.[5]

Another technique of law enforcement is the use of trained dogs. Dogs can sniff out illegal fish, game, and firearms that poachers may have thrown from vehicles during a chase. In addition, dogs can help law enforcement officers track poachers through wilderness areas.[6]

STING OPERATIONS

In addition to the practices already mentioned, federal and state agents often run undercover—better known as sting—operations. To do this they assume false identities and pose as guides, buyers, or hunters. Sometimes agents set up fake businesses such as interior decorating stores, pet stores, taxidermy shops, and establishments that outfit hunters. Agents sometimes use listening devices and hidden cameras to record illegal business transactions. Undercover operations may require that agents join hunting expeditions with people allegedly engaged in illegal activities. Carrying out a sting operation from start to finish may take months or even years, partly because it requires winning the trust of suspected criminals. This method, however, enables agents to obtain evidence against people believed to be involved in wildlife crime.

Some lawyers argue that sting operations are tantamount to entrapment, that is, encouraging people to break the law in order to prosecute them for it. They claim it is unfair for officers of the law to set traps, lie to suspects, and claim to be what they are not in order to bring charges against a suspect. The courts, however, have given great latitude to enforcement agencies in their undercover work. Defendants rarely are successful by arguing that they are the victims of entrapment.

Sometimes conservationists protest government sting operations, especially those involving endangered species or otherwise-protected animals. They object to the killing of protected animals as a way to catch poachers. Such action reduces the animals' numbers. In addition, they say that when agents purchase or hunt such wildlife, lowering the supply, they end up increasing the demand by poachers because with fewer animals the price goes up. The result is increased poaching of already-decimated species.

In Atlanta, Georgia, in 1986, in an effort to stop a major poaching operation, undercover agents bought and sold 500 pounds of alligators, 2,000 pounds of venison, 2,500 pounds of raccoons, and 1,000 pounds of fish that included the endangered shortnose sturgeon. They also bought the eggs of endangered fish as well as the eggs and meat of the endangered sea turtles. This sting operation lasted nearly two years and resulted in the arrests and convictions of 100 people.[7]

In 1987 a special undercover investigation by the Wisconsin Department of Natural Resources began. Called Operation Gillnet, the investigation was an effort to stem the illegal harvesting of lake trout from lakes Superior and Michigan. The poaching had become so extensive that it threatened the entire species. Wisconsin undercover wardens set up the bogus Tri State Foods company. Posing as truck drivers, businesspeople, warehouse workers, wardens, investment bankers, and brokers, they bought 60,000 pounds of illegal fish from commercial fish catchers and fish dealers. In the end, state officials were able to stop the large-scale poaching and restore the species for sportfishing.[8]

In Salt Lake City, Utah, in 1991, federal agents established themselves as bogus interior decorators and developed connections with taxidermists and hunters in Utah and southern California. These "decorators" provided wildlife trophies for homes, offices, and restaurants. Agents called this sting Operation Wasatch, and as of late 1993, authorities had indicted numerous people accused of killing illegal species, taking animals out of season, and exceeding the limits on the numbers of animals that it was legal to take. Officials say that the illegal wildlife trade in Utah and California is a continuing problem that will take years to solve.[9]

SPECIAL AGENT LUCINDA SCHROEDER

In 1991 two special agents began building up their physical stamina in preparation for a sting operation in Alaska. For over a year they worked out daily in the gym, swimming and doing exercises such as lifting weights, walking and running on the treadmill, pedaling stationary bicycles, and climbing steps. The goal of this sting operation was to bring down a group of outfitters and guides who arranged numerous illegal hunts for wealthy clients, and they needed to be in top shape to do so.

When they felt strong enough to handle Alaska's grueling terrain, they posed as a married couple, hunters out for big Alaskan game. They contacted one of the outfitters under surveillance by the Fish and Wildlife Services, and arranged their hunting trip. This outfitter is referred to in this book as Butch Henderson, although that is not his real name. For several days as members of a group, they hunted with Henderson and got to know him as a "friend." Then, one cold evening as they were all sitting around a fire telling hunting stories, the undercover couple began to brag about their hunting skills. Each claimed to be a better hunter than the other. Henderson suggested that the couple settle their argument with a contest. They agreed, but to their dismay he then insisted that each member of the couple hunt separately. The woman believed that if she insisted as she had learned to, on remaining with her partner because of the danger of their becoming separated, she would blow their cover and probably cost them their lives. Without a moment's hesitation and despite the danger, Lucinda Schroeder, one of seven female special agents working for the U.S. Fish and Wildlife Service, agreed. Her partner was not happy with her decision, but he could do nothing about it.

Henderson flew Schroeder to a prime hunting area and left her alone on a glacier with only her camping supplies, including her tent, hunting gear, and a three-day supply of food. He was also the only one who knew her location and although he promised to return in three days, Schroeder worried that he might not. If Henderson suspected the truth, he might never come back for her.

She turned her face into the cold wind and pulled the hood of her down jacket tighter around her ears. As she watched the Cessna lift off, then disappear behind a distant cloud, she prayed he had believed her story.

For three days Schroeder hunted unsuccessfully. They were a grueling and lonely three days. She had to pretend to take the contest seriously, for Henderson circled overhead, keeping track of her every movement. Schroeder climbed up and down steep cliffs, grateful for the time she had spent strengthening her body. Despite her diligence, she was unable to find a suitable animal. She needed one big enough or rare enough to win the contest. When Henderson checked on her, she feigned impatience. Without hesitation he suggested that they track one by plane. Schroeder agreed. They circled the area together until she spotted an old elk with a large rack. "That's the one I want," she said. She knew she had to kill something and chose the one she did because it was past its prime and unlikely to reproduce.

Henderson selected the spot where the kill would take place, and the next day he drove the animal toward her. She dropped the elk with one shot. Then, still playing the part of the proud hunter, Schroeder helped Henderson load the carcass onto the plane. Together they flew back to camp, where she proudly took more pictures of Henderson, the old elk, and the airplane. Then calmly, four-foot-nine-inch (1.2 m), 108-pound (49 kg) Special Agent Schroeder "rolled the gold and made the pinch," that is, showed her badge and made the arrest.

When Henderson realized the ruse, the words that came out of his mouth were enough to make the dead elk smile. Although he was the size of a Green Bay Packer quarterback, he offered no resistance as she closed the handcuffs on his thick wrists. Her partner looked on with satisfaction.

The pictures she had taken would become evidence at Henderson's court appearance. Depending on the outcome of the trial, Henderson could have lost his guide and hunting licenses, his airplane, and all his gear, and received both a jail term and a fine. To reduce his penalty he plea-bargained and gave evidence against other Alaskan guides and outfitters.

Through the years, Special Agent Schroeder has received a great many citations, including Pincher of the Year awards from the U. S. Fish and Wildlife Service for her undercover work in capturing poachers. To Special Agent Schroeder, sting operations are "business as usual" in the government's efforts to end wildlife theft.[10]

SPECIAL AGENT DAVE HALL

Another special agent who has achieved notice in recent years is Dave Hall, a former Louisiana bar brawler turned conservationist, biologist, and law enforcement officer. According to his own account, he applied the skills he learned as a devilish young man who poached, to catching poachers.[11] His most noteworthy undercover operations have involved poachers of alligators, Alaskan game, and ducks.

In 1976 Hall assumed the identity of a buyer of American alligator skins. At that time American alligators were on the brink of extinction largely because of poaching. Alligator skins were selling for forty dollars apiece. Records showed that in a three-year period poachers had skinned over 127,000 alligators—half the estimated number of alligators in the United States at the time! Hall was determined to do what he could to stop the Louisiana trade and its most notorious thief, A. J. Caro.[12]

Hall knew that gathering enough evidence to put Caro in jail would be perilous work. He set up his cover carefully and worked day and night to win Caro's trust. Several times he came close to being discovered. When undercover agents blow their covers, they may not live to tell about it. Hall, however, was lucky. Although there were tense moments, his scheme and disguise were convincing. By working closely with other wildlife agents, Hall was able to catch Caro in the act of illegally selling alligator skins. Thus, this infamous poacher who bragged to Hall that he could earn as much as $4,500 a day selling alligator skins, a man who called alligator poaching "the best money on the bayou," found himself facing a jail term.[13]

It is here that the story of Hall began to take a twist. As part of a plea-bargaining agreement, Caro agreed to work with Hall in catching other alligator poachers. Hall, like all law-enforcement officers, knew that the majority of lawbreakers will do almost anything to lower their fines or lessen their jail time. Hall just carried the arrangement one step further and developed a program he called Poacher to Preacher.

His idea was to convert poachers into crusaders for ethical hunting. In the course of several years, Hall convinced additional wildlife thieves to give up poaching, join his cause, and encourage their peers to hunt legally. A. J. Caro was his first poacher-turned-preacher, and others followed.

Ron Hays, for example, was one of Alaska's biggest bear poachers and according to Hall, the number-one enemy of the Alaska Game Department. Among other poaching methods, Hays routinely used his airplane to drive grizzlies toward hunting parties. Word of his willingness to do this spread far, and hunters from many places around the world traveled to Alaska where with Hays's assistance they killed trophy-sized sheep; bears such as grizzlies, and caribou. Hays was arrested for poaching in 1980: The government took away his guide license and his airplane and fined him $25,000. Yet, despite the conviction, Hays continued his illegal hunting. In 1986 he was arrested again and that time was jailed.

Hall visited Hays in prison and convinced him to make a thirty-minute video about the consequences of poaching. For his cooperation, Hays was released from jail. Hall, however, was not satisfied and wanted Hays to do more. He persuaded Hays to talk to groups of hunters about the effects of wildlife crime, and soon Hays became another crusader against illegal and unethical hunting.[15]

In addition to Hays, Hall has enlisted convicted duck hunters into his Poacher to Preacher program. In a plea-bargaining agreement, Dennis Treitler, a fourth-generation Louisiana duck poacher, agreed to make a video for Hall. As the tape rolls, the audience can hear Treitler confess to killing ducks by the thousands, hunting deer at night, and killing protected animals such as alligators and night herons—always ignoring the law. He then urges others not to do the same thing. He maintains that if hunters continue to kill at the rate at which they have been killing, nothing will remain for the next generation.[15] His words and manner are believable, and because of Hall's encouragement, he is convincing.

Once the video was made, Treitler thought his debt to society had been paid, but Hall had additional plans for the former poacher. He convinced Treitler to address the Ducks Unlimited International Waterfowl Symposium in Washington, D.C.

Treitler was reluctant to do this but agreed when a lawyer helped him. A "prominent lawyer in New Orleans bought me a suit—tailor made! and shoes.... It was the first suit I ever owned. Freaked me out. I only wore it once. I'm scared to death of it," said Treitler.[16]

When he finished his speech he got a standing ovation. "It was better than all the illegal ducks I ever killed. It was the greatest feeling in the world—and I have Dave Hall to thank," said Treitler.[17] Now Treitler speaks regularly to hunting groups about poaching.

Hall's Poacher to Preacher program is neither nationwide nor formal. It is simply one federal agent's effort to make a difference in the battle against poaching. Hall had indicated he'd rather do business with poachers than chase them. "Protecting wildlife isn't a job with me.... It's a religion," he said.[18]

SOURCE NOTES

CHAPTER ONE
1. "Jobless Rate and Poaching Rise in Timber Country," *New York Times,* 10 June 1982, sec. L, p. 39.
2. Marc Margolis, "Pantanal Poachers," *Christian Science Monitor,* 21 March 1983, p. 12.
3. "Indochina Refugees Accused of Poaching on the Coast," *New York Times,* 14 August 1980, sec. A, p. 18.
4. "Old War, Old Habits," *New York Times,* 9 August 1982, sec. A, p. 14.
5. Douglas D. Hoskins, southeast district warden, law enforcement supervisor, State of Wisconsin Department of Natural Resources, Milwaukee, Wisconsin, interviewed by author, 16 September 1992.
6. Margolis, 12.
7. Ken Slocum, "The Game Is at Stake as Wardens Combat a Plague of Poachers," *Wall Street Journal,* 4 May 1987, sec. A, p. 1.
8. Slocum, sec. A, p. 1.
9. Tony Horwitz, "Very Dark Plots Are About in England, as Grouse Grow Fat," *Wall Street Journal,* 18 October 1991, sec. A, p. 1.
10. Slocum, sec. A, p. 1.
11. Slocum, sec. A, p. 1.
12. Constance J. Poten, "America's Illegal Wildlife Trade: A Shameful Harvest," *National Geographic,* September 1991, 120–121.
13. Thomas Dunlap, *Saving America's Wildlife* (Princeton: Princeton University Press, 1988), 5, 177.
14. Sue Armstrong, "Cutting the Rhino's Losses," *International Wildlife,* January/February 1990, 24.
15. Kim Heacox, "The View from Zimbabwe," insert in article Robert F. Jones, "Farewell to Africa," *Audubon,* September 1990, 91.

16. Armstrong, 24.
17. Judy Mills, "I Want to Eat Sun Bear," *International Wildlife,* January/February 1991, 43.

CHAPTER TWO
1. Lisa Mighetto, *Wild Animals and American Environmental Ethics* (Tucson: University of Arizona Press, 1991), 2–5.
2. Thomas Dunlap, *Saving America's Wildlife* (Princeton: Princeton University Press, 1988), 10.
3. Mighetto, 30.
4. Mighetto, 30.
5. Mighetto, 32.
6. John F. Reiger, *American Sportsmen and the Origins of Conservation* (New York: Winchester Press, 1975), 90.
7. Reiger, 105.
8. Reiger, 119.
9. "Greed, Guns, Wildlife," *The World of Audubon.* See also Mark Cherrington, "Poaching: Beating Swords into Ploughshares," *Earthwatch,* October 1989, 26.

CHAPTER THREE
1. Patricia Brennan, "Audubon's Jarring Look at Poaching in America," *Washington Post,* 9 July 1989, TV Week section, p. 8.
2. Jane E. Brody, "Boom in Poaching Threatens Bears Worldwide," *New York Times,* 1 May 1990, sec. C, p. 11.
3. Constance J. Poten, "America's Illegal Wildlife Trade: A Shameful Harvest," *National Geographic,* September 1991, 110, 119; Steven Levingston, "Poachers Have Gall Killing Black Bears in United States Hinterlands," *Wall Street Journal,* 22 November 1988, sec. A, p. 17.
4. Brody, sec. C, p. 11.
5. Levingston, sec. A, p. 17.
6. Jack Anderson and Dale Van Atta, "Asian Folk Remedies Endanger U.S. Bears," *Washington Post,* 15 November 1991, sec. E, p. 3.
7. Brody, sec. C, p. 1.
8. Sean Kelly, "Setting CITES on Gallbladder Trade: Demand for Bear Organs in Eastern Cultures Spurs Poaching in North America," *Washington Post,* 2 March 1992, sec. A, p. 3.
9. Levingston, sec. A, p. 17.
10. Poten, 114.
11. Kelly, "Setting CITES on Gallbladder Trade," sec. A, p. 3.
12. "Poaching Operations Found Killing Bears for Aphrodisiac Use," *New York Times,* 26 January 1989, sec. A, p. 8.

13. Anderson and Van Atta, "Asian Folk Remedies," sec. E, p. 3.
14. Poten, 112.
15. Brody, sec. C, p. 1.
16. Sean Kelly, "Wildlife Biology: Poaching Bears for Asian Market," *Washington Post,* 26 August 1991, sec. A, p. 2.
17. Judy Mills, "I Want to Eat Sun Bear," *International Wildlife,* January/February 1991, 43.
18. Brennan, TV Week section, p. 8.
19. Daniel Glick, "The New Killing Fields," *Newsweek,* 23 July 1990, 4.
20. Anderson and Van Atta, "Asian Folk Remedies," sec. E, p. 3.
21. "43 Are Accused of Poaching Black Bears for Body Parts," *New York Times,* 25 August 1988, sec. A, p. 20.
22. Glick, 55.
23. Donald L. Rheem, "Poaching in U.S. Worsens as Demand Grows," *Christian Science Monitor,* 24 April 1987, 1; Anderson and Van Atta, *Washington Post,* 15 November 1991, sec. E, p. 3.
24. "Greed and Wildlife: Poaching in America," A National Audubon Society Specials series, PBS Video, 1988.
25. Brody, sec. C, p. 11.
26. Lucinda D. Schroeder, special agent, United States Department of the Interior, United States Fish and Wildlife Service, Division of Law Enforcement, Madison, Wisconsin, interviewed by the author, 18 September 1992.
27. Rheem, 6.
28. Brennan, TV Week section, p. 8.
29. Poten, 114.
30. Michael Milstein, "The Quiet Kill," *National Parks,* May/June 1989, 24.
31. Wayne Pacelle, "Fund Campaigns to Save Bears," *Fund for Animals. Fund for Animals* is the newsletter of the Fund for Animals.
32. Milstein, 24.
33. William Dicke, "Increased Poaching Is Reported by Many States," *New York Times,* 31 October 1982, sec. L, p. 42.
34. Glick, 4; Poten, 124.
35. Poten, 124; Glick, 55.
36. Glick, 55.
37. Poten, 124.
38. Schroeder, interview.
39. Poten, 131.
40. John Balzar, "Sting Breaks Up Slaughter of Alaska Wildlife," *Los Angeles Times,* 15 February 1992, sec. A, p. 26; Michael Tennesen, "Poaching, Ancient Traditions and the Law," *Audubon,* July/August 1991, 93.
41. Poten, 131.

42. Jack Anderson and Dale Van Atta, "America's Ivory Hunters," *Washington Post,* 25 February 1990, sec. B, p. 7; See also "Walrus-Headhunting Ring Uncovered in Alaska, U.S. Agents Say," *New York Times,* 15 February 1992, sec. L, p. 6; sec. A, p. 26.
43. Balzar, sec. A, p. 1.
44. Anderson and Van Atta, "America's Ivory Hunters," sec. B, p. 7.
45. Ken Slocum, "The Game Is at Stake as Wardens Combat a Plague of Poachers," *Wall Street Journal,* 4 May 1987, sec. A, p. 1.
46. Poten, 124.
47. Milstein, 124; Dicke, sec. L, p. 42.
48. Slocum, sec. A, p. 1.
49. Poten, 124.
50. "A Step Over a Property Line: A White-tailed Deer Carcass and a $250 Fine," *New York Times,* 10 December 1990, sec. B, p. 2; "White-Tailed Deer: Creatures or Crops?" Hunting Fact Sheet #2, Fund Facts, n.d. Fund Facts is a series of information sheets produced by the Fund for Animals.
51. Rheem, 1.
52. Greg Sefton, "The Noble Assassins," *Southern Outdoors,* January-February, 1976, 22; Schroeder, interview. Douglas D. Hoskins, southeast district warden, law enforcement supervisor, State of Wisconsin Department of Natural Resources, Milwaukee, Wisconsin, interviewed by author, 16 September 1992.
53. "Poachers Said to Kill Starving Deer in West," *New York Times,* 24 January 1984, sec. A, p. 8.
54. "A Step Over a Property Line," sec. B, p. 2.
55. "A Step Over a Property Line," sec. B, p. 2.
56. "Officers Find Poached Deer in Freezer Raid," *New York Times,* 21 November 1988, sec. B, p. 3.

CHAPTER FOUR

1. Ted Gup, "Trail of Shame," *Time,* 16 October 1989, 66.
2. Nick Worrall, "Uganda Wildlife Faces Extinction by Poachers," *Christian Science Monitor,* 24 June 1980, 10; Alan Cowell, "African War Pits 2 Against an Army," *New York Times,* 25 December 1981, sec. A, p. 2.
3. Paul Van Slambrouck, "How Unique Is a Slim Elephant with Huge Feet?" *Christian Science Monitor,* 10 February 1982, 2.
4. Thomas W. Netter, "Ivory Quotas Reduce Poaching of Elephants," *New York Times,* 27 May 1986, sec. C, p. 4; "Kenya Moves to Stop Poaching of Elephants," *New York Times,* 9 October 1988, sec. A, p. 25.
5. Dan Freeman, *Elephants: The Vanishing Giants* (New York: G. P. Putnam's Sons, 1981), 165.

6. Worrall, 10.
7. Jay Ross, "The Guns of Revolution Make War on Africa's Elephant Herds," *Washington Post,* 13 December 1982, sec. A, p. 17.
8. Gup, 68.
9. Van Slambrouck, "How Unique Is a Slim Elephant?" 2.
10. Paul Van Slambrouck, "Poachers from Mozambique," *Christian Science Monitor,* 7 December 1982, 1.
11. "Wildlife for Sale," Know Zone series No. 13, WGBH-TV, Boston, 1988.
12. "Kenyan Patrols Find 924 Elephant Tusks," *New York Times,* 17 March 1985, sec. A, p. 20.
13. Jane Perlez, "Besieged Elephants Find Ally," *New York Times,* 6 September 1988, sec. A, p. 1.
14. Mary Battiata, "Poaching of Wildlife called 'Out of Control,'" *Washington Post,* 3 November 1988, sec. A, p. 1.
15. Battiata, "Poaching of Wildlife," sec. A, p. 1.
16. Battiata, "Poaching of Wildlife," sec. A, p. 1.
17. Mary Battiata, "Game Parks Fall Prey to Neglect," *Washington Post,* 14 February 1988, sec. A, p. 1.
18. Robert F. Jones, "Farewell to Africa," *Audubon,* September, 1990, 51–104; Neil Henry, "Preserving Paradise in Kenya," *Washington Post,* 4 September 1989, sec. A, p. 20.
19. Richard Littell, "Culling Ivory, Saving Elephants," *Washington Post,* 23 February 1989, sec. C, p. 5.
20. Mark Cherrington, "Poaching: Beating Swords into Ploughshares," *Earthwatch,* October 1989, 25.
21. "U.N. Conference Bars Ivory Imports," *Washington Post,* 17 October 1989, sec. A, p. 13.
22. Colman McCarthy, "Saving Elephants: This Year's Cause," *Washington Post,* 19 August 1989, sec. A, p. 19.
23. Jane Perlez, "Two-legged Rogues Are on the Run," *New York Times,* 11 February 1989, A4; Jones, p. 52.
24. Gup, 68–69; Nathan M. Adams, "The Elephants' Last Chance," *Reader's Digest,* July 1990, 47–50.
25. Jay Ross, "Elephant Slaughter Chills a Park's Peace," *Washington Post,* 19 December 1982, sec. A, p. 46.
26. Gup, 66–73.
27. Glenn Frankel, "Black Rhinos Face Extinction," *Washington Post,* 23 June 1985, sec. A, p. 16
28. Frankel, sec. A, p. 16.
29. *Wall Street Journal,* "Death in Zimbabwe," 10 October 1990, sec. A, p. 14.
30. Jane Perlez, "Rhino Near Last Stand, Animal Experts Warn," *New York Times,* 7 July 1992, sec. A, p. 5.

31. Frankel, sec. A, p. 16.
32. Perlez, "Rhino Near Last Stand," sec. A, p. 5.
33. Frankel, sec. A, p. 16.
34. Alan Cowell, "In Rhino Country: A Fight to Save Horns of Africa," *New York Times*, 5 September 1983, sec. L, p. 2.
35. Frankel, sec. A, p. 16.
36. Judy Mills, "I Want to Eat Sun Bear," *International Wildlife*, January/February 1991, 40.
37. John F. Burns, "Medicinal Potions May Doom Tiger to Extinction," *New York Times*, 15 March 1994, sec. B, p. 5.
38. Malcolm W. Browne, "Folk Remedy Demand May Wipe Out Tigers," *New York Times*, 22 September 1992, sec. B, p. 9.
39. "The Police in India Confiscate the Bones of Some 20 Tigers," *New York Times*, 7 September 1993, sec. A, p. 4.
40. Browne, sec. B, p. 9.
41. Suzanne Possehl, "Russians and Americans Team Up to Save Endangered Tiger," *New York Times*, 31 August 1993, sec. B, p. 7; Browne, sec. B, p. 9.
42. Burns, sec. B, p. 5.
43. Possehl, sec. B, p. 7.

CHAPTER FIVE

1. "The Destruction of Our Nation's Waterfowl," "Hunting Fact Sheet #3," *Fund Facts*, n.d. *Fund Facts* is a series of information sheets produced by the Fund for Animals.
2. *The Illegal Duck Hunt. Waterfowl for the Future: Status of Ducks, 1988. Crackdown on Waterfowl Baiters.* Made for United States Fish and Wildlife Services by Thomson Vanduch Production, Bookings, South Dakota. Lent to the author courtesy of Lucinda D. Schroeder, special agent, United States Department of the Interior, United States Fish and Wildlife Service, Division of Law Enforcement, Madison, Wisconsin.
3. Joe Skorupa, "Outdoors: High-Tech War on Poachers," *Popular Mechanics*, July 1990, 31.
4. Lucinda D. Schroeder, special agent, United States Department of the Interior, United States Fish and Wildlife Service, Division of Law Enforcement, Madison, Wisconsin, interviewed by the author, 18 September 1992.
5. "The Destruction of Our Nation's Waterfowl."
6. *The Illegal Duck Hunt*, 1988.
7. "210 Waterfowl Hunters Charged After U.S. Inquiry into Poaching," *New York Times*, 14 December 1988, sec. A, p. 24; *The Illegal Duck Hunt*.
8. *The Illegal Duck Hunt*, 1988.

9. *The Illegal Duck Hunt,* 1988.
10. *The Illegal Duck Hunt,* 1988.
11. Denis Elliott, "IWLA Helps Bag Nongame Bird Poachers in Louisiana," *Outdoor Ethics,* Vol. 10, No. 1. Winter 1991: 6. *Outdoor Ethics* is the newsletter of the Izaak Walton League of America.
12. Denis Elliott, p. 6.
13. Constance J. Poten, "America's Illegal Wildlife Trade: A Shameful Harvest," *National Geographic,* September 1991, 110.
14. *The Illegal Duck Hunt,* 1988.
15. Elliott, "IWLA Helps Bag Nongame Bird Poachers," 6.
16. Elliott, "Four Receive Jail," 7.
17. Gregory Septon, a taxidermist at the Milwaukee Public Museum, Milwaukee, Wisconsin, interviewed by the author, 14 October 1993.
18. Schroeder, interview.
19. "Illegal Wildlife Bring High Prices," *New York Times,* 3 April 1985, sec. A, p. 17; Septon, interview.
20. Interview with Ralph E. Christensen, director, Bureau of Law Enforcement, Division of Enforcement, State of Wisconsin Department of Natural Resources, Madison, Wisconsin, 5 October 1992.
21. Philip Shabecoff, "Warrants Issued for Slayers of Eagles Over Eight States," *New York Times,* 16 June 1983, sec. A, p. 18.
22. Shabecoff, sec. A, p. 18.
23. Poten, 127.
24. Schroeder, interview.
25. Schroeder, interview; Michael Tennesen, "Poaching, Ancient Traditions and the Law," *Audubon,* July/August 1991, 93.
26. Schroeder, interview.
27. Tennesen, 93.
28. Schroeder, interview; Shabecoff, sec. A, p. 18.
29. Schroeder, interview.
30. Schroeder, interview; Poten, 110.
31. Poten, 127.
32. John Nichol, *The Animal Smugglers and Other Wildlife Traders* (New York: Facts on File, 1987), 35.
33. Nichol, 20, 22.
34. Nichol, 50.
35. Nichol, 52.
36. Nichol, 19, 20, 83.
37. Nichol, 78.
38. Nichol, 82.
39. Nichol, 167–171.
40. Diane Galusha, "Falconry: Sport of Kings or Sport of Thieves?"

Outdoor Ethics, Vol. 6, No. 1 (winter 1987): 1; *Outdoor Ethics* is the newsletter of the Izaak Walton League of America. "Illegal Wildlife," sec. A, p. 17.
41. Nichol, 7, 22.
42. Nichol, 106.

CHAPTER SIX

1. Douglas D. Hoskins, southeast district warden, law enforcement supervisor, State of Wisconsin Department of Natural Resources, Milwaukee, Wisconsin, interviewed by the author, 16 September 1992; Ralph E. Christensen, director, Bureau of Law Enforcement, Division of Enforcement, State of Wisconsin Department of Natural Resources, Madison, Wisconsin; interviewed by author, 5 October 1992.
2. Interview with Dennis Kirschbaum, conservation warden, Department of Natural Resources, Prairie Du Chien, Wisconsin, 21 December 1992.
3. Christensen, interview.
4. Kirschbaum, interview.
5. Wallace Turner, "U.S. Agency Finds Indian Poachers Peril Salmon," *New York Times,* 28 July 1982, sec. A, p. 18.
6. Farley Mowat, *Sea of Slaughter* (Boston: Atlantic Monthly Press, 1984), 184.
7. Constance J. Poten, "America's Illegal Wildlife Trade: A Shameful Harvest," *National Geographic,* September 1991, 118.
8. Frank Murkowski, "Save the Salmon from Poachers," *New York Times,* 4 March 1989, sec. A, p. 27.
9. Dan Morain, "Salmon Smuggling Ring Cracked: Asian Firms, Individuals Indicted," *Los Angeles Times,* 13 April 1989, sec. I, p. 32.
10. David Sanger, "North Pacific Poaching Arrests Have Tokyo Squirming," *New York Times,* 30 May 1990, sec. A, p. 3; "North Pacific Dispute," *Wall Street Journal,* 1 June 1990, sec. A, p. 12.
11. Scott Heard, special agent, U.S. Fish and Wildlife Service, Madison, Wisconsin, interviewed by author, 18 September 1993.
12. Poten, 116.
13. Poten, 129.
14. Lance Frazer, "Lethal Trade: Illegal Collecting Jeopardizes Reptiles," *Outdoor Ethics* Vol. 9, No. 1 (winter 1990): 1. *Outdoor Ethics* is the newsletter of the Izaak Walton League of America.
15. Frazer, 7.
16. Frazer, 1, 7–8.
17. John Nichol, *The Animal Smugglers and Other Wildlife Traders* (New York: Facts on File, 1987), 23, 24, 30, 32.

18. Marc Margolis, "Pantanal Poachers," *Christian Science Monitor,* 21 March 1983, 12.
19. Frazer, 7.
20. Frazer, 7.
21. "Beware: Sea Turtle Product Imports are Prohibited!," *World Wildlife Fund—Focus,* May/June 1993, 3.
22. "For Turtles, Man Is Threat," *New York Times,* 11 July 1988, sec. A, p. 12.
23. Poten, 110; Karen Karvonen, "Crucial Clues," *Outdoor Ethics* Vol. 10, No. 1 (winter 1991): 7. *Outdoor Ethics* is the newsletter of the Izaak Walton League of America; Ellen Kort, Appleton, Wisconsin, interviewed by the author, 26 March 1993.
24. Jacqueline Wiora Sletto, "Unlikely Victims: Poaching Puts Plants in Peril," *Outdoor Ethics,* Vol. 11, No. 3 (summer 1992): 3. *Outdoor Ethics* is the newsletter of the Izaak Walton League of America.
25. Christensen, interview.
26. Richard W. Risch, conservatory director, Milwaukee County Department of Parks, Recreation and Culture, Milwaukee, Wisconsin, interviewed by the author, October 1992.
27. Risch, interview.
28. Sletto, 3.
29. Robert Reinhold, "For Rustlers, Cactus Is the Big Cash Crop," *New York Times,* 30 August 1987, sec. E, p. 4.
30. Laurie M. Grossman, "Developing a Triffid-Sized Variety Should Take Care of the Poachers," *Wall Street Journal,* 7 August 1991, sec. B, p. 1.
31. Timothy Eagan, "Carving Out a Market for Oregon's Yew Tree," *New York Times,* 31 May 1991, sec. A, p. 12.
32. Ivars Peterson, "Poachers Are Felling Trees for Seasonal Profits," *New York Times,* 15 December 1991, sec. 1, p. 47.
33. Peterson, 47.

CHAPTER SEVEN

1. Lisa Mighetto, *Wild Animals and American Environmental Ethics* (Tucson: University of Arizona Press, 1991), 29.
2. Wayne Pacelle, "Wildlife Mismanagement," *The Animals' Agenda,* September 1991, 14.
3. "China is Said to Arrest 203 for Panda Poaching," *New York Times,* 7 April 1988, sec. A, p. 13.
4. Jane E. Brody, "Boom in Poaching Threatens Bears Worldwide," *New York Times,* 1 May 1990, sec. C, p. 1.
5. Constance J. Poten, "America's Illegal Wildlife Trade: A Shameful Harvest," *National Geographic,* September 1991, 114.

6. Jack Anderson and Dale Van Atta, "The Poaching Boom," *Washington Post,* 22 December 1991, sec. C, p. 7.
7. Jack Anderson and Dale Van Atta, "America's Ivory Hunters," *Washington Post,* 25 February 1990, sec. B, p. 7; "Elephant Ivory Trade," Traffic, USA, August 1990. Traffic, USA, is a series of fact sheets produced by the World Wildlife Fund.
8. Poten, 124.
9. Michael Satchell, "The American Hunter Under Fire," *U.S. News & World Report,* 5 February 1990.
10. Sue Armstrong, "Cutting the Rhino's Losses," *International Wildlife,* January/February 1990, 23.
11. Marian Gitlin Newman, Letter to the Editor, *New York Times,* 20 May 1983, sec. A, p. 31.
12. Charles Wallace, "A Wildlife Smuggler's Paradise," *Los Angeles Times,* 20 October 1990, sec. A, p. 31.
13. John Nichol, *The Animal Smugglers and Other Wildlife Traders* (New York: Facts on File, 1987), 97.
14. Wallace, 31.
15. Ralph E. Christensen, director, Bureau of Law Enforcement, Division of Enforcement, State of Wisconsin Department of Natural Resources, Madison, Wisconsin, interviewed by the author, 5 October 1992.
16. Mary Battiata, "Poaching of Wildlife Called 'Out of Control,'" *Washington Post,* 3 November 1988, sec. A, p. 1.
17. Jane Perlez, "Kenya's Government Fights for Control in a War That Endangers Tourism," *New York Times,* 27 August 1989, sec. E, p. 2; "Death in Zimbabwe," *Wall Street Journal,* 10 October 1990, sec. A, p. 14.
18. Angus Phillips, "130 Accused of Unlawful Wildlife Sales," *Washington Post,* 17 January 1985, sec. A, p. 3.
19. Lucinda D. Schroeder, special agent, United States Department of the Interior, United States Fish and Wildlife Service, Division of Law Enforcement, Madison, Wisconsin, interviewed by the author, 18 September 1992.
20. Robert F. Jones, "Farewell to Africa," *Audubon,* September 1990, 51–104; Marc Reisner, *Game Wars: The Undercover Pursuit of Wildlife Poachers* (New York: Viking Press, 1991), 160-63.
21. Wallace, sec. A, p. 1; Nichol, 18–19, 74–85.

CHAPTER EIGHT

1. Ken Slocum, "The Game Is at Stake as Wardens Combat a Plague of Poachers," *Wall Street Journal,* 4 May 1987, sec. A, p. 1; Douglas D. Hoskins, southeast district warden, law enforcement supervisor; State of Wisconsin Department of Natural Resources,

interviewed by the author, Milwaukee, Wisconsin, 16 September 1992.
2. Charles Askins, "Poachers Slaughter While America Watches," *Petersen's Hunting,* August 1977, 26–27.
3. Rick Mooney, "Wake Up Calls: Anti-Poaching Hotline Users Help Nab Game Law Violators," *Outdoor Ethics,* Vol. 9, No. 4, (fall 1990): 4. *Outdoor Ethics* is the newsletter of the Izaak Walton League of America.
4. Press Release, National Audubon Society, 1 November 1991.
5. Mooney, 4.
6. Mooney, 5.
7. Hoskins, interview, September 1992.
8. Hoskins, interview.
9. "Field Notes," *Outdoor Ethics,* Vol. 11, No. 2 (spring 1992): 2. *Outdoor Ethics* is the newsletter of the Izaak Walton League of America.
10. Denis Elliot, "IWLA Helps Bag Nongame Bird Poachers in Louisiana," *Outdoor Ethics,* Vol. 10, No. 1 (winter 1991): 6. *Outdoor Ethics* is the newsletter of the Izaak Walton League of America.
11. Ted Williams, "Open Season on Endangered Species," *Audubon,* January 1991, 32.

CHAPTER NINE
1. "Poaching," n.d., National Parks and Conservation Association. "Poaching" is a press release.
2. Timothy M. Beardsley, "Fowl Play: A U.S. Agency Uses Science to Fight Wildlife Bandits," *Scientific America,* October 1990, 28; Barry Meier, "Tracing Illegal Ivory: Forensic Scientists Take on Smugglers," *New York Times,* 29 October 1991, sec. C, p. 4.
3. Meier, sec. C, p. 4.
4. Daniel Glick, "A Scotland Yard for Crimes Against Animals," *Newsweek,* 23 July 1990, 4.
5. Gary Scovel, "The Decoy," *The Facets of Wisconsin's Warden Force,* September/October 1987, 23.
6. Larry Miller, "Continuing Education for Conservation Wardens," *The Facets of Wisconsin's Warden Force,* September/October 1987, 9.
7. "Game Wardens Arrest 100 As Poachers," *New York Times,* 23 May 1986, sec. A, p. 10.
8. Larry Kriese, "Great Lakes Patrol," *The Facets of Wisconsin's Warden Force,* September/October 1987, 20–21.
9. John Lancaster, "Governments Crack Down on Poaching for Profit," *Washington Post,* 2 May 1991, sec. A, p. 3.
10. Lucinda D. Schroeder, special agent, United States Department

of the Interior, United States Fish and Wildlife Service, Division of Law Enforcement, Madison, Wisconsin, interviewed by the author, 18 September 1992.
11. Jim Darnell, "From Poacher to Preacher," *Texas Outdoor Writers Association Monthly Newsletter,* February 1992. March Reisner, *Game Wars: The Undercover Pursuit of Wildlife Poachers* (New York: Viking Penguin, 1991) has a full account of Dave Hall and his activities.
12. W.P. "Commercial Wildlife Killing 20th Century Style, A Review of *Game Wars: The Undercover Pursuit of Wildlife Poachers* by Marc Reisner," *The Animals' Agenda,* September 1991, 16.
13. W.P., 16.
14. "Convicted Poachers Enlisted to Save Big Game of Alaska," *New York Times,* 26 December 1990, sec. A, p. 28.
15. Susan Reed, "Fighting Fire with Fire," *People,* 17 June 1991, 86; *The Illegal Duck Hunt,* 1988. Made for United States Fish and Wildlife Services by Thomason Vanduch Production.
16. Reed, 90.
17. Reed, 86.
18. Ken Slocum, "The Game Is at Stake as Wardens Combat a Plague of Poachers," *Wall Street Journal,* 4 May 1987, sec. A, p. 1.

FOR FURTHER READING

BOOKS

Douglas-Hamilton, Iain and Oria. *Among the Elephants.* New York: Viking Press, 1975.

Freeman, Dan. *Elephants: The Vanishing Giants.* New York: G. P. Putnam's Sons, 1981.

Mighetto, Lisa. *Wild Animals and American Environmental Ethics.* Tucson: University of Arizona Press, 1991.

Mowat, Farley, *Sea of Slaughter.* Boston: Atlantic Monthly Press, 1984.

Nichol, John. *The Animal Smugglers and Other Wildlife Traders.* New York: Facts on File, 1987.

Reiger, John F. *American Sportsmen and the Origins of Conservation.* New York: Winchester Press, 1975.

Reisner, Marc. *Game Wars: The Undercover Pursuit of Wildlife Poachers.* New York: The Viking Press, 1991.

ARTICLES

Adams, Nathan M. "The Elephant's Last Chance." *Reader's Digest,* July 1990, 46–52.

Armstrong, Sue. "Cutting the Rhino's Losses." *International Wildlife,* January/February 1990, 22–24.

Beardsley, Timothy M. "Fowl Play: A U.S. Agency Uses Science to Fight Wildlife Bandits." *Scientific American,* October 1990, 28.

Cherrington, Mark. "Poaching: Beating Swords into Ploughshares." *Earthwatch,* October 1989, 22–29.

Glick, Daniel. "The New Killing Fields." *Newsweek,* 23 July 1990, 4 and 55.

Gup, Ted. "Trail of Shame." *Time,* 16 October 1989, 66–73.

Jones, Robert F. "Farewell to Africa." *Audubon,* September 1990, 51–104.
Mills, Judy. "I Want to Eat Sun Bear." *International Wildlife,* January/February 1991, 38–43.
Milstein, Michael. "The Quiet Kill." *National Parks,* May/June 1989, 19–25.
Milstein, Michael. "Slaughter in Our National Parks." *Reader's Digest,* April 1990, 122–125.
Poten, Constance J. "America's Illegal Wildlife Trade: A Shameful Harvest." *National Geographic,* September 1991, 106–132.
Skorupa, Joe. "Outdoors: High-Tech War on Poachers." *Popular Mechanics,* July 1990, 30–31.
Tennesen, Michael. "Poaching, Ancient Traditions and the Law." *Audubon,* July/August, 1991, 90–97.
Williams, Ted. "Open Season on Endangered Species," *Audubon,* January 1991, 26–35.

INDEX

Africa, 19, 48–60, 93–94
Alaska, 38, 42, 119–21, 123
Alligators, 79, 85, 111, 118, 122
Animal mistreatment, 96–97
Animal rights movement, 25
Antlers, 39–40, 46
Arizona, 34, 85, 88
Arkansas, 74
Asia, 32–33, 48
Asians, in U.S., 10, 68
Australia, 75, 96

Back hoe, 80
Bald eagle, 72
Bears, 19, 31–38, 93, 111, 123
Bighorn sheep, 43–44, 94
Birds, 15, 19, 22–23, 63–78, 93, 96, 110
    legislation, 26–27, 30
Bird trappers, 76, 78
Bolivia, 85
Boone and Crockett Club, 24
Borneo, 62
Brazil, 14, 85
Buffalo, 92
Burundi, 55
Butterflies, 20

Cacti, 88–89
California, 35, 85, 88, 119
Caviar, 84
Central African Republic, 58
China, 32–33, 38, 57, 61, 93
Christmas trees, 90–91
CITES, *see* Convention on International Trade in Endangered Species
Clams, 79–81
Colorado, 38, 40
Connecticut, 34, 46
Conservation movement, 24–25
    organizations, 108–10
Convention on International Trade in Endangered Species (CITES), 28, 30, 53–55, 74, 84, 98

Decoys, 116–17
Deer, 15–16, 44–47, 107
Desert plants, 88
Dogs
    bear hunting, 36
    law enforcement, 117
Douglas-Hamilton, Iain, 49–50
Dubai, 57

Ducks, 63–64, 66, 68, 93, 100, 123–24
Ducks Unlimited, 66

Eagles, 70–72, 111
Earth First!, 92
East African Wildlife Society, 52
Ecosystem, 100–101
Education, wildlife, 110
Eggs, 63, 68, 70, 87, 118
Elephants, 48–57, 93–94, 96, 111
Elk, 39–40, 116, 120–21
Endangered Species Act, 28, 83
Eskimos, 41–43

Falconry, 68–70
Feathers, 70–72, 74
Federal Migratory Birds Act, 27
Fish, 20, 81–84, 97–98, 118–19
Fish and Wildlife Service, U.S., 28, 36, 38, 71–72, 109–10
Florida, 34, 38, 106
Food, 22–23
　birds, 63, 74
　meat, 34, 44
　turtles, 84

Gall, bear, 32–35, 38, 111
Gallbladder, bear, 32–36, 38, 93
Game farms, 38, 40
Geese, 107–8
Germany, 74, 90
Giant pandas, 62, 93
Gibbon, 96
Gila monster, 85
Ginseng, 87–88
Great Smoky Mountains National Park, 25, 38, 93
Grizzly bears, 34, 93, 108

Hall, Dave, 121–24
Hawks, 69–70
Hide, see Skin and hide
Hong Kong, 53, 57, 60
Horns, 43, 57–58, 60, 94–96
Hunting, 21–26
　attitudes toward, 98–100
　bears, 35–36, 38
　waterfowl, 64, 66–67
　see also Market hunting; Sport hunting

Illinois, 107
Indiana, 48, 57, 61
Indonesia, 74–75, 98
International trade, 28, 98
　elephant ivory, 50, 53–57, 116
　ginseng, 87
　rhinoceros horns, 60
　salmon, 83
　tigers, 61
Interstate shipping, 26
Ivory
　elephant, 49–50, 52–57, 111, 116
　rhinoceros, 57–58
　walrus, 41–43
Izaak Walton League of America, 108, 110

Japan, 33–34, 53–54, 57, 83, 85, 87
Jewelry, 34, 43, 50, 87

Kabalega National Park, Uganda, 49–50
Kangaroo, 96
Katmai National Park, 38
Kenya, 52–53, 97
Kruger National Park, South Africa, 50

140

Lacey Act, 26, 83
Lead shot, 64
Leakey, Richard, 52–53
Legislation, 26–30
Louisiana, 14, 64, 66, 74, 93, 110, 122

Mammals, 19
Marine Mammal Protection Act, 28
Market hunting, 22, 24, 26, 31, 44
Massachusetts, 34
Medicinal products, 32, 39–40, 60–61
Mescaline, 88
Mexico, 74–75, 88–89
Migratory Birds Treaty, 26–27
Minnesota, 106
Mississippi, 74
Monkeys, 60, 96
Montana, 9, 35, 40
Mozambique, 50
Murkowski, Frank, 82

Namibia, 50, 55, 94
National Antipoaching Foundation, 106
National Audubon Society, 38, 93, 108
National Fish and Wildlife Foundation, 110
National parks and forests, 24–25
Native Americans, 70–72, 81–82
Nebraska, 72
Nevada, 85
New Guinea, 74–75
New Jersey, 90
New Mexico, 85, 103, 105, 116
New York, 34, 46
Night hunting, 46–47

North Carolina, 90
North Korea, 32, 38, 83

Oklahoma, 85
Ooziks, 42
Operation Bicornis, 94
Orangutans, 61–62, 93–94
Oregon, 35, 81, 90
Organized crime, 98
Owls, 70
Ownership of land and wildlife, 25–26

Panthers, 61
Paraguay, 85
Passenger pigeons, 92
Pearls, 80–81
Pee Glow Elk case, 116
Plants, 19, 79, 87–91
Poacher to Preacher program, 122–24
Poaching, 12–20
    definition, 11–12
    effects, 92–101
    reasons for, 18–19, 79
Polluted waters, 80–81, 97
Protected species, 26–28, 30

Ranthambhor National Park, India, 61
Raptors, 68–72
Red tides, 80
Reilly, William K., 93
Reptiles, 19, 79, 84–87
Rewards, 105–6, 108
Rhinoceroses, 19, 57–60, 93–95
Roadhunting, 116–17
Rocky Mountains, 39, 93
Roosevelt, Theodore, 24–26
Russia, 61
    see also Soviet Union

Salmon, 79, 81–83
Saudi Arabia, 70
Save the Elephant Summer, 55, 103
Schroeder, Lucinda, 119–21
Sea creatures, 19, 28
Shells, clam, 80
Sikhote-Alin Nature Reserve, Siberia, 61
Singapore, 55, 75
Skin and hide, 34–35, 61
Smuggling, 97
    birds, 63–64, 75–76
    cacti, 89
    elephant tusks, 55
    rhinoceros horns, 60
Snakes, 85
Somalia, 53, 55
South Africa, 50
South Carolina, 90
South Dakota, 72
South Korea, 32–34, 38
Soviet Union, 82–83
    see also Russia
Sport fishing, 84
Sport hunting, 23–24, 39, 53, 99, 102
Sting operations, 117–22
Sudan, 53, 58
Sumatra, 62

Taiwan, 57
Tanzania, 53, 55, 57
Taxidermy, 74
Taxol, 90
Texas, 68, 85, 88
Thailand, 19, 75, 85, 96–98
Tigers, 61
Tortoiseshell, 87

Trade, see International trade
TRAFFIC (Trade Records Analysis of Flora and Fauna in Commerce), 108
Trees, 87, 90–91
Trophies, 94, 119
    bears, 34, 36
    bighorn sheep, 43
    deer, 46
    elk, 39
Turtles, 84–85, 87, 118

Uganda, 49–50, 53, 58
Undercover operations, 117–22
United Arab Emirates, 57
Utah, 119

Venus's-flytrap, 89–90

Walrus, 40–43
Washington, 35–36, 72
Waterfowl, 64–68
Wild Bird Conservation Act, 30
Wildlife Conservation International, 55
Wildlife Forensics Laboratory, U.S., 113–16
Wildlife sanctuaries, 48, 50, 61
Willamette National Forest, 90
Wisconsin, 68, 72, 107, 118
World Wildlife Fund, 49, 55, 62, 93–94, 108

Yellowstone National Park, 24, 39
Yemen, 58, 60

Zambia, 94
Zimbabwe, 19, 58

Emmaus High School Library
Emmaus, Pennsylvania

WITHDRAWN

42541

364.162 GRE

Greene, Laura Offenhartz.
Wildlife Poaching.